HISTORY IN ACTION

England in the Middle Ages

Chris Jordan

Queen Elizabeth's School and
Community College, Crediton

Tim Wood

John Murray

HISTORY IN ACTION   Chris Jordan and Tim Wood

Already published

The Ancient World

Old World, New World 1480–1600

In Preparation

The Modern World

All artwork by Susan Bird.

Acknowledgements

The authors are particularly grateful to Terry Fiehn, head of the history department at Parliament Hill School, London, for his advice and help.

Illustrations

Aerofilms Ltd, 6 (left, centre and right), 46, 49; J. J. Bagley from *Life in Medieval England*, 38; The BBC Hulton Picture Library, 24 (bottom), 48, 51 (top and bottom), 56; Bodleian Library, 20 (top and bottom); The Bodley Head (from *London's River* by Eric de Maré), 4 (top); Janet and Colin Bord, 18; The British Library, 5, 22, 24 (top), 45; The Fitzwilliam Museum, 52 (top) and cover; The Mansell Collection, 14, 27, 63, 64; The National Gallery, 52 (bottom); Wayland Picture Library, 4 (bottom); graph from *Life, Marriage and Death in a Medieval Parish* by Zvi Razi (Cambridge University Press), 63.

Sources for quoted passages

p.4: 'Exeter in the 12th Century' (Acts of Stephen), 'London in 1150' (William FitzStephen), and 'London in 1200' (Richard of Devizes), quoted in *Portraits and Documents: The Early Middle Ages*, ed. Derek Baker (Hutchinson).

p.28: 'Of the Sports of London' (William FitzStephen), quoted in *English Historical Documents*, ed. D. C. Douglas (Eyre and Spottis-woode).

p.53: 'Advice to an earl to build a castle manned by monks against Satan' (from *Odericus Vitalis: Historia Ecclesiastica*, ed. A. le Provost 1838-55, ii 417-20) and 'Kidnapping of schoolmaster by friars' (from *Registres d'Innocent IV*, no 529), quoted in *Western Society and the Church* by R. W. Southern (Pelican).

p.57: *The Magnificent Century* by Thomas B. Costain (Tandem).

p.61: Michael of Piazza, quoted in *The Black Death* by Johannes Nohl (Unwin Books).

p.62: Agnolo di Tura, quoted in *The Black Death* by P. Ziegler (Penguin); 'The Black Death in the Monasteries' (from *Chronicon Angliae* by Thomas of Walsingham) and 'The Black Death in Florence' (Giovanni Boccaccio), quoted in *The Black Death and Peasants' Revolt* by L. W. Cowie (Wayland Documentary History).

© Chris Jordan and Tim Wood 1984

First published 1984
by John Murray (Publishers) Ltd
50 Albemarle Street, London W1X 4BD

Pupils' Book reprinted 1985, 1986, 1987, 1988
Teachers' Book reprinted 1988

Printed and bound in Great Britain at The Bath Press, Avon

British Library Cataloguing in Publication Data

Jordan, Chris
    England in the Middle Ages,—(History in action)
    Pupils' book
    1. Great Britain—History—Medieval period,
    1066-1485
    I. Title   II. Wood, Tim   III. Series
    942.03   DA175

    ISBN 0-7195-3955-2

Jordan, Chris
    England in the Middle Ages,—(History in action)
    Teachers' book
    1. Great Britain—History—Medieval period,
    1066-1485
    I. Title   II. Wood, Tim   III. Series
    942.03   DA175

    ISBN 0-7195-4095-X

Contents

First Impressions

Medieval London (drawing from a wood-cut)

Exeter in the Twelfth Century

'Exeter is a large city, ranking they say, the fourth in England. It is surrounded by ancient Roman walls and is famous for its fisheries, for abundance of meat, and for its trade and commerce. Its castle stands on a tall mound protected by impregnable walls, and towers of stone.'

London in 1150

'Those engaged in business of various kinds, sellers of merchandise, hirers of labour, are distributed every morning into their several localities according to their trade. Besides, there is in London on the river bank among the wines for sale in ships, and in the cellars of the wine-merchants a public cook-shop. There daily you may find according to the season, dishes of meat, roast, fried and boiled, large and small fish, coarser meats for the poor and more delicate for the rich such as venison and big and small birds.'

London in 1200

'Every race of men out of every nation . . . go there in great numbers; every country has brought its bad habits and bad manners. No one lives there without being affected; there is not one street without miserable and filthy people; there the worse you behave, the better you will get on. . .'

Use these pictures and documents to help you answer these questions:

1 Choose some of the words from this list to write a sentence about medieval towns:

poor; large; crowded; rich; empty; clean; small; noisy; dirty; smelly; quiet.

2 Describe 2 ways in which medieval towns were different from modern towns.

3 Describe 2 ways in which medieval towns were similar to modern towns.

4 What might have been some of the advantages and disadvantages of living in a medieval town?

Medieval street scene

English Towns in 1300

It is difficult to know how many people lived in the main towns during the Middle Ages. Many tradespeople drifted back to the countryside and there was no national census (a properly organised count of everyone in the country). However, we can get some idea of the size and importance of English towns from records of taxation. The more taxes paid by a town the more important it was.

The following table shows the amount paid by various towns as the tallage tax in about 1300. (Tallage tax was a tax on the number of people in a town.)

TOWN	TAX PAID	SIZE ON MAP
London	450 marks	10 mm square
Lincoln	120 marks	5 mm square
Winchester	120 marks	5 mm square
Canterbury	90 marks	4 mm square
Worcester	75 marks	3 mm square
Oxford	75 marks	3 mm square
York	65 marks	3 mm square
Marlborough	45 marks	2 mm square
Norwich	45 marks	2 mm square

1 Trace the outline map of England and Wales into your books.

2 Using an atlas, mark in the positions of the towns shown on the table above.

3 Draw a square box (the sizes are shown on the table above) for each town on the map to show its relative importance.

Paying taxes to the King's collector

5

Maintown

Towns grew up in England as centres of trade and industry. They developed during late Saxon times (from about AD 1000). When William I (William of Normandy) became King in 1066, he had to try to protect the most important towns from attack by English and Scottish rebels, to show that he could control England.

Look carefully at the map of Maintown opposite. This is an imaginary English town in about 1080. Study the facts below.

Maintown

Maintown is the most important centre in northern England. It was founded in Saxon times and is a large port. It is a place where a number of important routes cross and many ships call there. The river forms a natural defensive barrier to the north. There are a number of industries in Maintown which produce large amounts of woollen cloth, leather goods, armour and swords. These are particularly useful to the Normans. Maintown is also a trading centre and many goods are sent by road and sea to London. A great deal of the wool is sent abroad in ships and the town contains a number of rich merchant families. About 1000 people live in Maintown and there are several smaller towns and villages nearby within a day's walking distance.

The Normans

The Normans are very good architects and builders. Probably the best way to defend the town would be to build a castle like one of those in the pictures. The castle should be near the main communication points like the bridges, roads, rivers and tracks. It would need firm foundations because it would be strongly built out of stone. Often the walls would be 1 or 1½ metres thick.

Building a Norman castle

The Latest News

Attacks have been made on the town from across the border. Rebels are collecting foreign ships and money for a possible invasion of the whole area by sea.

1 Choose one of the sites A to E shown on the map to build a castle. Write a short paragraph saying why the other sites are unsuitable.

2 Write a paragraph giving your reasons for defending Maintown.

3 Draw a picture of Maintown Castle. Library books will help you.

The Defence of Maintown

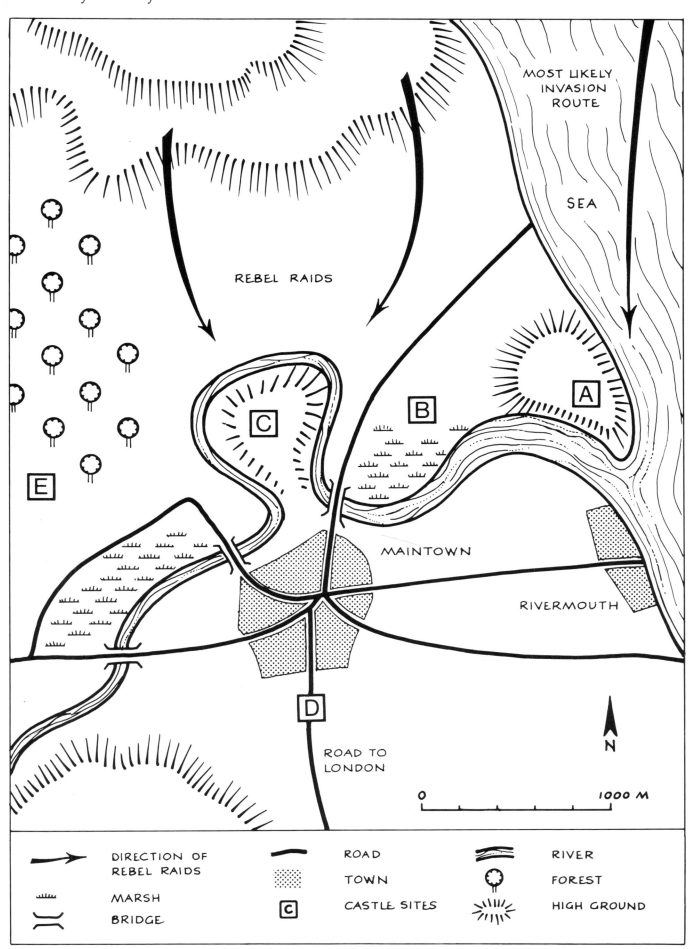

Maintown in 1300

Towns continued to grow and prosper in England under the firm rule of William I and the Norman kings.

Study the plan of Maintown opposite. Answer the following questions.

1 List five differences between Maintown in 1300 and a modern town.

2 What clues can you find in the plan that Maintown was (a) a trading centre, (b) a religious centre, (c) a market town?

3 List the streets where you would have been able to buy the following goods: a loaf of bread; food for your horse; eggs; a horseshoe; meat; an iron pot; spices; a belt.

4 Count the number of streets where shops or trades would have been. What do you think was the most important trade in Maintown?

Copy the following passage into your books, filling in the blanks. (The plan will help you.)
Then explain in your own words why and how the townspeople and the villagers needed one another.

Medieval towns were collections of houses and streets surrounded by a . . . .
   Raw materials (A) such as . . . . or . . . . were brought into the town from the villages and farms.
   Craftsmen then turned these materials into finished goods (B) such as . . . . or . . . . These goods were carried into and out of the town along the . . . . or the . . . . Most towns would therefore have several main . . . .
   A . . . ., inside or outside the walls, would protect the town.

The Wool Trade

Wool was the most important trade in England in 1300. You will see from the diagram that most wool was sent abroad. The King made a great deal of money from taxes on the wool trade.

SENT TO FLANDERS TO BE WOVEN INTO HIGH QUALITY CLOTH

BOUGHT BY MERCHANTS

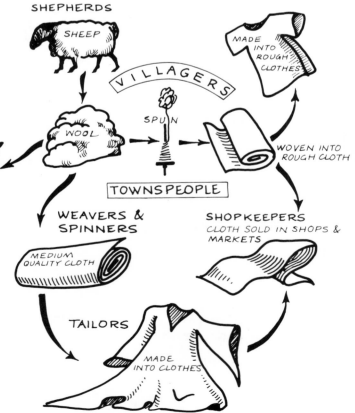

SHEPHERDS

SHEEP

VILLAGERS

MADE INTO ROUGH CLOTHES

SPUN

WOOL

WOVEN INTO ROUGH CLOTH

TOWNSPEOPLE

WEAVERS & SPINNERS

SHOPKEEPERS
CLOTH SOLD IN SHOPS & MARKETS

MEDIUM QUALITY CLOTH

TAILORS

MADE INTO CLOTHES

1 Use the diagram to write a short account of how the wool trade worked in 1300.

2 Who do you think, out of all the people shown on the diagram, made the most money from the wool trade? Explain your answer.

3 Use the diagram and the plan of Maintown to explain the importance of the wool trade to Maintown in 1300.

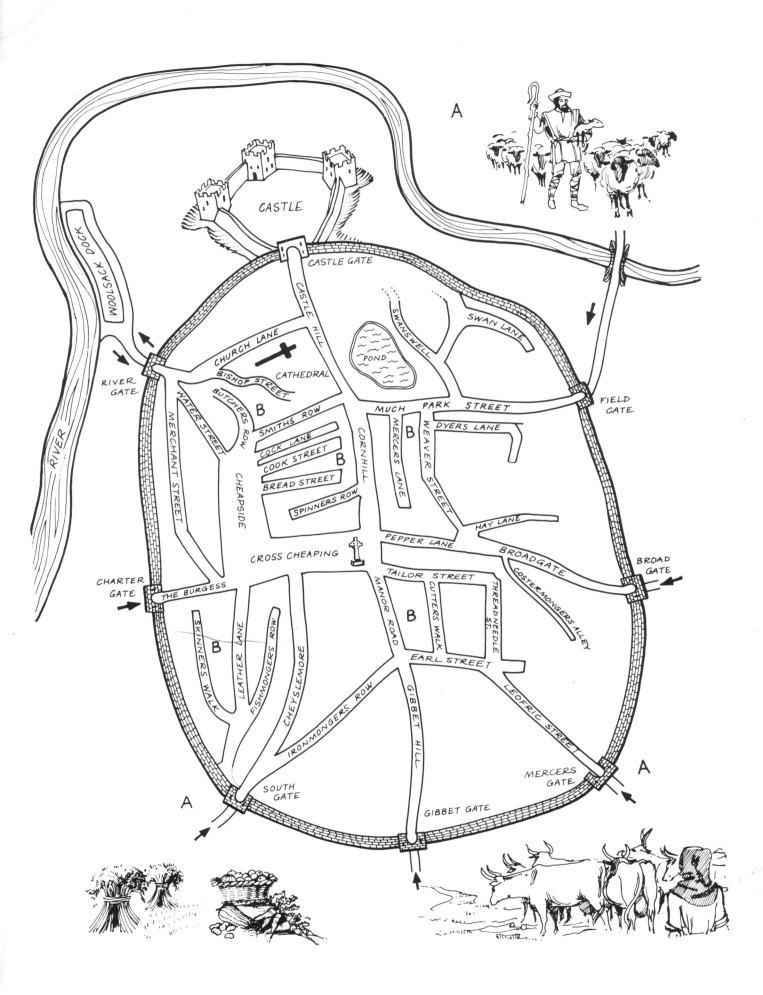

CASTLE

CASTLE GATE

WOOLSACK DOCK

RIVER GATE

CASTLE HILL

CHURCH LANE

BISHOP STREET

CATHEDRAL

SWANSWELL POND

SWAN LANE

FIELD GATE

RIVER

MERCHANT STREET

WATER STREET

BUTCHERS ROW

B

SMITHS ROW

COCK LANE

COOK STREET

BREAD STREET

SPINNERS ROW

CHEAPSIDE

CORNHILL

MUCH PARK STREET

MERCERS LANE

B

WEAVER STREET

DYERS LANE

B

HAY LANE

PEPPER LANE

BROADGATE

BROAD GATE

COSTERMONGERS ALLEY

CHARTER GATE

THE BURGESS

CROSS CHEAPING

SKINNERS WALK

B

LEATHER LANE

FISHMONGERS ROW

CHEYSLEMORE

IRONMONGERS ROW

MANOR ROAD

TAILOR STREET

CUTTERS WALK

THREADNEEDLE ST.

EARL STREET

B

GIBBET HILL

LEOFRIC STREET

MERCERS GATE

A

SOUTH GATE

A

GIBBET GATE

9

The Charter

Towns often grew up on the land of great noblemen (called barons) who taxed the townspeople and governed the town. Once a town had been established for some time, its citizens could try to buy a *charter* from the King. This would be expensive, but the townspeople would gain three major rights:

(a) the right to build walls around the town;

(b) the right to elect aldermen to make laws for the town;

(c) the right to fix their own prices and local taxes.

Not all the citizens agreed that a charter was worthwhile. Consider the arguments for and against, then make up your own mind. Explain your decision.

William de Brun, Master Tailor

Owns a large shop in the town and two large houses

Otto, Beggar (wounded in war)

Lives in a small hut just outside the town

William's main points in favour of buying a charter:

1 The walls will make the town safe, especially at night. There are many bandits, outlaws and rebels.

2 It will be easier to keep a record of inhabitants and traders if the town gates can be closed. This will keep out strangers and undesirable people. Keeping records will mean that cheats and thieves will be caught more easily.

3 It is much better to be ruled by local people than by a nobleman who lives on a country estate miles away, and spends most of his time fighting in foreign lands or travelling around with the King's court. He knows nothing of the problems of the townspeople.

4 Many of the taxes we pay now go straight to the nobleman and are not used for the town at all.

5 The King will recognise the town as being very important.

6 Trade will increase. Traders will send their goods to the town market because it will be safe.

Otto's main points against buying a charter:

1 Many small houses on the edge of town will have to be pulled down to build the wall. Many poor townspeople live in this area.

2 The price of bread and other food will go up and already most poor people can only afford one loaf of bread a week.

3 The King cannot be trusted. He could take the money and then refuse to grant the charter.

4 The charter will be very expensive to buy. This will mean more taxes for the poor to pay.

5 The walls will have to be manned by soldiers. These soldiers will have to be either hired or else pressed into service. If they are hired they will be strangers and will have no love for the town or the townspeople. If they are pressed they will be resentful. In any case these armed men may cause trouble by throwing their weight around. They may start arresting poor people and accusing them of being thieves or beggars.

6 The gates will be closed at night and people will be locked out. Poor people who cannot afford to live inside the town will get no protection.

Streets in Medieval Towns

Study the Scene Below

1 Give four reasons why this street was not a healthy place.

2 List three points about the way the houses are built that would mean that fire would spread quickly.

3 Would you say the street was overcrowded? Explain your answer.

4 How did house-owners get rid of their rubbish?

5 Why would the traders be interested in keeping the streets clean?

6 Why were each of the following wandering in the streets?
(a) pigs   (b) dogs   (c) rats

7 What were the advantages (if any) of having animals wandering in the streets? What were the disadvantages?

8 Produce a report by a modern health inspector on a medieval town.

Houses

Look at the picture below. It shows a row of timber-framed houses built for merchants in Maintown in the Middle Ages. Space was short in towns, so houses were packed tightly together. The biggest and most impressive houses belonged to the richest and most important people. A few rich people had houses built of stone.

Design a Medieval House

All members of the class can design their own medieval house. The picture above may give you some ideas. Start by drawing a grid of 1-cm squares. Make it 13 cm square. You will draw your house on the grid.

The class is divided into four groups of house-owners. The teacher will give money to each member of the class according to the table below.

1 Rich merchants . . . . 250 units
2 Traders . . . . 150 units
3 Shopkeepers . . . . 120 units
4 Townspeople . . . . 80 units

You use this money to design a house using the following materials (*not all of them have to be used*):

BEAMS	These were essential in most medieval houses, as they were built by the timber-frame method already described.
PLASTER	This was essential and was used for the outside walls.
ROOF	This was made of wood or thatch. On a larger house it would be made from tiles. You can save money by making your house narrower and the roof steeper.
WINDOWS	These were made from leaded glass and were very expensive.
DOORS	These were made from wood, studded with iron. The larger the better.
EXTRAS	You can add decorations to your house. These can be fancy lead, rosettes, shields, carvings or other forms of ornamentation.

The diagram on the right shows how most town houses were built in the fourteenth century. Large wooden beams were fitted together to make a framework. The spaces in between were filled in with thin twigs or sticks woven together (wattle). This was covered on both sides by a plaster made from mud and straw (daub), which was coated with lime plaster to make it waterproof.

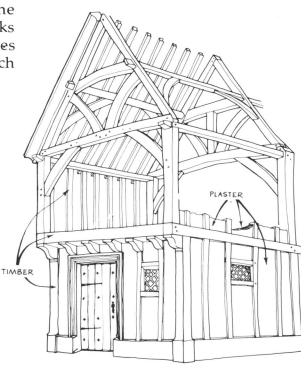

PRICES OF MATERIALS (per square)

WHOLE ROOF (THATCH)	WHOLE ROOF (TILES)	BEAMS	PLASTER	EXTRAS	DOOR	LEADED GLASS
1	2	½	1	3	2	3

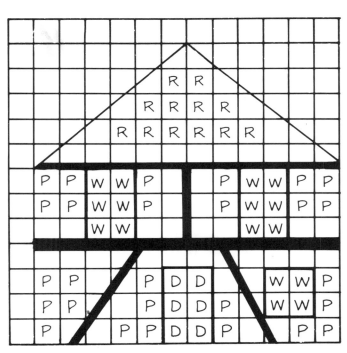

- Only draw the front of the house
- Part squares do not count—except for beams and windows and doors
- Decorations can only be added to plaster or beams already paid for
- Study the example below before you start

Door (D)	$6 \times 2 =$	12
Beams	$40 \times ½ =$	20
Roof (R)	$12 \times 2 =$	24
Plaster (P)	$27 \times 1 =$	27
Windows (W)	$16 \times 3 =$	48

$\overline{\underline{131}}$ { Suitable for traders

When you have finished you can put all the houses together to make a frieze to go round the classroom and make your own medieval street. Colour and draw in all the parts of the house properly. The drawings above may give you some ideas.

Markets and Fairs

Markets

Many medieval towns held regular markets, when traders would set up tables or stalls in the centre of town. People would come in from the countryside to buy or sell.

The stallholders had to pay a fixed amount of money (stallage) to the town council or aldermen and agree to be honest and fair traders. Most markets were checked regularly by officials who measured and weighed produce with a standard set of weights and measures. People bringing goods into the market, like salt, leather or iron, would have to pay a toll or tax before they could sell or exchange them.

As well as this regular market, there were specialist markets on certain days—fish markets, corn markets or cloth markets. Market days were very busy indeed and attracted large crowds into the town.

Market stalls

Customs of the City of Winchester

(24) . . . no butcher or other man may have a stall in the High Street without paying the due to the city.

(30) . . . every cart that comes into the city with fish for sale . . . owes to the King's rent one half-penny.

(49) . . . every cart that brings iron or steel twopence, a horseload one penny.

(52) . . . every cart that brings tanned leather for sale owes twopence, a horseload one penny.

(60) . . . every tanner that holds a stall in the High Street of Winchester owes for the ground which he takes up two shillings a year.

Fairs

A fair would be held once a year in certain large towns or cities which were situated on important trade routes.

Merchants and money-lenders from all over Europe travelled to the fairs to buy and sell, fix contracts or exchange money. The great fair at Troyes in France lasted a month and had three main stages. The first was a cloth fair. Traders came to show and buy samples of linen, woollens and silks. Prices were agreed for all types of cloth. (Undyed cloth was the cheapest and scarlet cloth was the most expensive.)

During the next stage of the fair, goods like spices, dyes, grain or wine were weighed out in fixed amounts and sold to the highest bidder. Peppercorns were a very popular item sold in this part of the fair. Merchants were often cheated by traders who made peppercorns of clay or flour.

The last part of the fair was a period of money-changing and lending by bankers and merchants.

1 Draw a picture of a market stall.

2 Explain what was meant by 'stallage' and 'tolls'.

3 Why is the stall in the picture *outside* the walls of the town?

4 Explain why traders found it easy to sell their goods at a market.

5 Give three reasons why the people who lived in the town would have liked a market to be held there.

6 Explain what a fair was.

7 Give three main differences between a market and a fair.

8 Copy and complete this map. First write in the names of the three regions of Europe in the boxes marked A, B, C. Then, using the table opposite, write the name of any one trade good which travelled along each route numbered 1 to 5 (e.g. write Wool along route 1).

TRADE BY REGION

REGION	EXPORT	IMPORT
ENGLAND	WOOL	WINE
FLANDERS	CLOTH	WOOL
CHAMPAGNE	WINE	CLOTH
ARAGON	LEATHER	CLOTH
LOMBARDY	SPICES	CLOTH

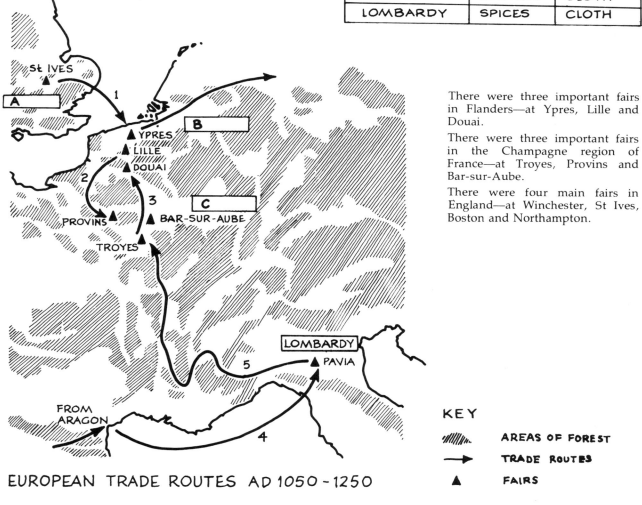

EUROPEAN TRADE ROUTES AD 1050-1250

KEY
////// AREAS OF FOREST
→ TRADE ROUTES
▲ FAIRS

There were three important fairs in Flanders—at Ypres, Lille and Douai.

There were three important fairs in the Champagne region of France—at Troyes, Provins and Bar-sur-Aube.

There were four main fairs in England—at Winchester, St Ives, Boston and Northampton.

9 Explain why Italian money-lenders and merchants spent several months in Flanders and Champagne.

10 Explain why Flanders was a rich and important area in medieval Europe.

11 Write a paragraph explaining whether Maintown should hold a market or a fair. Look closely at the map; think about the work you have completed on Maintown and trade.

15

Crime and Punishment

Medieval towns were rough, violent places. It was often unsafe to be out on the streets after dark. For this reason, most large towns had a *curfew*—that is, no one would be allowed to enter the town or walk around from sunset to dawn. Some of the most common criminals were called 'bruisers' or 'common night walkers'.

The aldermen would appoint a Common Sergeant who patrolled the streets at night, and checked that all the town's bye-laws were being kept to during the day.

It is important to remember that towns had been established for protection, and in 1351 all citizens of London were forbidden to wear arms within the city walls. In 1339, 29 people had been killed in London in fights or quarrels (although this total includes two drunks who fell into the Thames while trying to find their way home).

The aldermen and judges felt that violent crime should be matched by violent punishment: so criminals were frequently whipped, mutilated or put to death. Thieves or burglars were hanged; house-breakers were often buried alive; traitors were hanged, drawn and quartered.

The purpose of punishment was that the convicted person should never be able to repeat the crime. So a pickpocket might have his hand cut off; a runaway servant might be crippled. Fines were a common form of punishment and they were often so heavy that the criminal would choose to go to prison rather than pay.

The account rolls for the City of London tell us a good deal about crime and punishment, since the aldermen were involved in administering justice and collecting fines and expenses.

The Criminals

1 You have been caught trying to sell a silver cup and plate that have been missing from the local parish church for several weeks.

2 You have refused the King's order to attend archery practice, or to supply the local council with two bows and twenty arrows so that they can arm the town in case of attack.

3 Three witnesses have reported you as a scold. They say that you have refused to cook meals for your husband, you have shouted at him in the street, and dragged him out of the local ale-house.

4 You have borrowed a large sum of money from a wealthy shop-owner. You find you cannot repay the money, and you have been caught trying to sneak out of town late at night.

5 You have been caught leaving Chormley Hall, a large house owned by the richest merchant in town. The door had been broken down, the servants beaten up, and the money chest smashed. You were found with several gold coins hidden in your purse.

6 You have been found by the Common Sergeant bending over a dead body with a knife in your hand. The body was that of your neighbour and business rival, who had recently run off with your daughter.

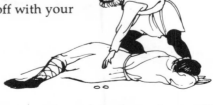

7 You are a servant, and you have been detained by the Common Sergeant for walking the streets, singing, shouting and kicking doors after the 7 o'clock curfew.

8 You guard the main gates to the town. You have been caught sleeping at your post on a night when robbers entered the town by climbing the walls.

In 1368, John Halliwell, a journeyman, was fined 40 marks for running off with his master's wife; Alice Shether was placed in the stocks for an hour for 'repeatedly defaming, molesting and backbiting her neighbours'. In 1385, three servants were imprisoned because 'they went wandering about Billingsgate about the 11th hour of the clock'.

Many of the town's bye-laws were sensible regulations about health, hygiene and living conditions. Traders would be told to move their rubbish out of the streets, and the town council would test selected goods (bread and wine, for instance) using official weights and measures kept in the town hall. Carts with iron-rimmed wheels were not allowed to break up the streets; farmers were responsible for any of their own animals that wandered through the streets.

In addition, the aldermen had to remember the royal commands and laws, the common law of England and the religious feelings and orders of the Church. They had a wide range of powers. They could use torture to extract evidence. Gradually, the aldermen's decisions became established as a set of rules so that criminals and judges knew what punishment was usually given. But there were few hard and fast rules, and little chance of appeal.

The class is divided into four or five groups. Each one represents a group of aldermen judging certain criminals in Maintown.

1 Each group should study carefully the list of possible punishments and the illustrations explaining them. Ask your teacher to explain anything that is not clear.

2 The teacher gives each group three or four criminals from the list on page 16. The judges must then decide, by discussion, on a suitable punishment for each criminal.

3 Each group must produce an illustrated account explaining the crimes they tried; the punishments they gave; why they made their decisions and what they feel will be the effects of their decisions.

Possible Punishments

1 Put in the stocks or pillory for 24 hours.

2 Made to march through the main streets of the town, being whipped by two men with leather lashes.

3 Thrown over the town walls (10 feet high) by two men. Told never to return.

4 Hand cut off.

5 Nose slit (would not prevent breathing or cause death).

6 Ear cut off and nailed to the market cross in the centre of the town.

 7 Branded on forehead with red-hot iron: 'C' for criminal.

8 Sent to prison 'at the King's pleasure' (no fixed number of years).

9 Buried alive outside the town.

10 Hanged on the local gibbet (gallows).

11 Fined 5 shillings (3 months' wages for most people).

12 Told to leave town.

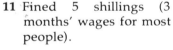

13 Put in ducking-stool and ducked in the river for two minutes.

14 Given a free pardon.

15 Take an oath on the Bible not to repeat the crime.

The Guilds

From the plan of Maintown you will have seen that tradespeople tended to build their shops very close together, often in the same street. This could create problems.

Study the drawing and answer the questions opposite.

1 Suggest why all the bakers' shops (A-D) are in Bread Street.

2 If A charges 2p for a loaf of bread, what price will B have to charge to attract more customers?

3 Why is it better for all four bakers to agree to charge the same price for bread?

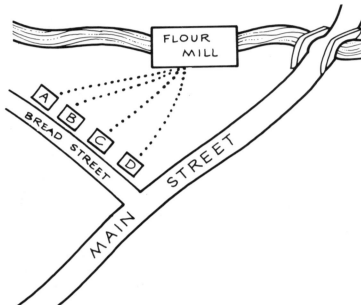

It was a great help if all the bakers joined together to fix the price of a loaf of bread. This association of bakers could also make important decisions about how and when to bake bread, when to sell it and when to hold special market days.

These trade associations were known as *guilds* in the Middle Ages.

The guilds tried to help their members when they had problems. They also provided entertainments and feasts, and kept an eye on the way business was done.

Some guilds became very rich and built large halls where the members could meet. This one is in Thaxted, Suffolk

The Bakers' Guild

Study the guild rules on this page carefully.

You are a member of the Bakers' Guild in Maintown in 1300.

1 Draw up a list of five rules for the Bakers' Guild. The following points should be covered: prices, hours of work, standard of bread, entertainments, insurance for injury.

2 Design a banner for the Bakers' Guild which will be paraded through the streets on feast days.

3 Suggest what action should be taken by the Guild in each of the cases below:

(a) *John Ball, baker.* Member of the Guild. He baked twelve loaves which were found to contain chalk dust and straw. One contained a dead mouse.

(b) *Ralf Brown, baker.* Member of the Guild. Ralf burnt his hand in one of his ovens. He will be unable to work again for a month.

(c) *Odo Verdun, merchant.* He is a trader from Belgium who wants to open a new shop selling Dutch bread, cheap but of poor quality.

(d) *James Whitehead, apprentice.* Several customers have complained that when they took their own dough to Whitehead's oven to be cooked, the quantity of bread they got back was too small. They assume Whitehead has been stealing dough to give to his master.

Rules of Other Guilds

Rules of The Bristol Weavers, 1346

1 Firstly, that no cloth be made unless it is six bondes in width. If anyone produces narrower cloth, let him be fined 40 pence.
2 If the threads in the cloth are too far apart, that cloth and the instrument on which it was worked to be burnt.
3 If any of the weavers work at night, let him be fined 5 shillings to the Mayor and 40 pence to the Alderman if he is found doing it a second time.

Rules of Lincoln St Michael Guild, 1349

1 On the death of a member of the Guild the banner of the Guild shall be brought to the house and carried before the body to the church.
2 On the eve of the feast of Corpus Christi, all members shall come together to the Guild Feast.
3 If any member fall ill and is unable to earn his living, he shall have, day by day, a penny from the members of his Guild.
4 If any member goes away from Lincoln for a year, and then seeks to rejoin the Guild, he must pay 12 pence.

Some guild badges

Dyers

Glovers

Stockfishmongers

Merchant Taylors

Grocers

The Bakery Game

Making dough and making loaves

This is a game about profits to be made from baking and selling loaves of bread. Bread is made by mixing flour, yeast and water to make a dough and then putting this dough into a hot oven. If yeast is left out, the bread remains flat and hard, but can still be eaten.

Each member of the class owns a baker's shop in Maintown and must decide how much bread to bake, what type of bread and how to make it. Bread is baked in a large tray which is placed in a hot oven as shown in the pictures above and below.

Selling bread

Making Your Bread

Each member of the class starts with a sum of 24 units to buy ingredients from the list below. Look at the list carefully and decide how you will spend your 24 units. The prices are all for a whole tray of bread. There are four shelves in the oven. One tray fills one shelf.

Ingredients	Cost per tray (units)
Wholemeal flour	5
Brown flour	3
White flour	2
Rough husk flour (for black bread)	2
Water	0

Additives per tray (no bread can contain more than 2)	
Yeast	1
Salt	1
Fruit	1
Milk	1
Chalk dust	−1
Bonemeal	−1
Straw	−1
Dust and pebbles	−1

Heating the Oven
(this is only counted *once* however many trays you bake)
If oven contains *any*

Wholemeal or black bread . . .	2 for oven
White or black bread	1 for oven

Hints on Baking

Look carefully at the table opposite. You may find ways of saving money, but remember you *must* sell your bread.

Selling Your Bread

The price of bread was fixed by law. This is shown in the table below.

> PRICE OF BREAD
>
> Bread was sold in four qualities. The prices shown below are for whole trays of bread.
>
> Wholemeal or fruit bread . . . . 8 units
> Brown bread . . . . 6 units
> White bread . . . . 4 units
> Rough black bread . . . . 3 units

Hints on Selling Bread

1 The more expensive the bread, the better the quality should be.
2 There is a limit to the amount of bread people can eat.
3 Think about the sort of customers you will have.

When you have made all your decisions, copy the score sheet below, fill it in and hand it to your teacher who will tell you how much of the bread you have made you will sell. The player with the biggest profit is the winner of the game.

Name:			
Loaf	Trays baked	Cost of ingredients	Heating costs
Wholemeal/fruit			These will be *either* 2 (if your oven contains any wholemeal or brown bread) *or* 1 if there is no wholemeal or brown bread.
Brown			
White			
Black			

Cost = ... + 2 or 1 (cross out the one you do not want)

= TOTAL COST . . . .(A)

I sell . . . . .trays for a total price of . . . . (B)

TOTAL PROFIT = Price received (B) − total costs (A)

My Total Profit is . . . . (B−A)

1 What did yeast do to the bread?

2 Why could yeast be left out of the black bread?

3 Which type of bread would have sold best in medieval towns? Why?

4 What advantages were there for the baker in using chalk dust, straw, dust and pebbles?

5 How would these additives have affected your reputation as a baker?

6 Rules were made about the quality of bread in medieval times, especially about the ingredients used. What benefits did this bring to (a) the customers, (b) the bakers?

7 Explain why you did not win the game.

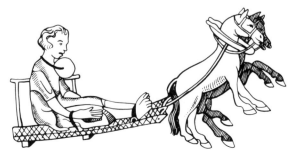

A dishonest baker is punished: he is dragged through the town on a hurdle with one of his bad loaves hanging round his neck

Apprentices 1

(See page T5 of the Teachers' Notes)

This is a board game to show some of the opportunities open to young men who moved into the towns hoping to find fame and fortune.

The playing board and list of moves are given opposite. Each pupil plays the game. The winner is the one with the highest score at the end of the game.

Moves

Pupils play by moving a counter or a suitable token (e.g. a small coin) from hexagon to hexagon.

Start with the counter on hexagon 1. You can move in any direction you like but:

1 You can move only one hexagon per round.
2 You can only enter each hexagon *once*, so take care not to be trapped.
3 You may not cross the heavy black lines. You can finish the game whenever you like (within the 30-minute playing period). You can make as many or as few moves as you wish.

Scoring

Make a copy of the score sheet. Each move you make and your score must be entered for each round.

To work out your score consult the table showing the list of moves. This shows what you are doing in life and the scoring for each hexagon.

Note

1 Some hexagons score no points.
2 Some hexagons score minus points because the activity would cost you a lot of money.
3 Some hexagons score plus points because the activity brings you benefits.
*4 The moves for hexagons 15 and 18 are called RISK. These may score plus or minus points. Your teacher will not tell you which you have scored until the end of the game. This is a risk you may wish to take.
5 Once you have landed on hexagon 15 you may either stay there or move on to 18. *No other move is allowed.*

Glassblowers' apprentices

22

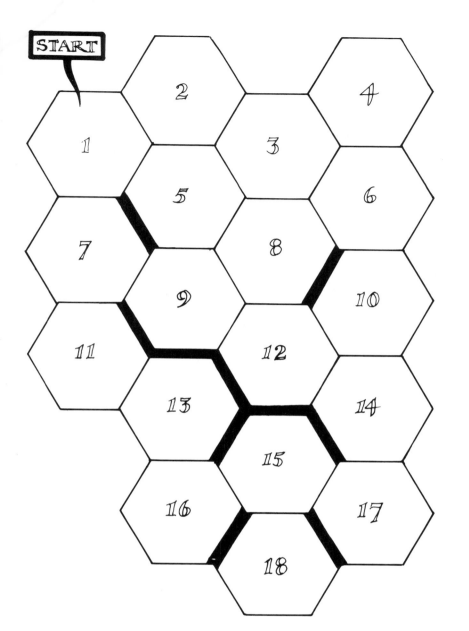

SCORESHEET		
ROUND	HEXAGON	SCORE
1		
2		
3		
4		
5		
6		
7		
8		
9		
10		
11		
12		
13		
14		
15		
16		
17		
18		
FINAL SCORE		

Advice

Before you begin, read the list of moves carefully and decide what kind of life you wish to lead. Bear in mind the dangers and rewards of medieval life.

List of moves

The number of the hexagon is followed by the action to be taken. The score is shown in brackets.

1 Move to London (0)
2 Take rooms in an inn (−2)
3 Go drinking (0)
4 Get a job in the fish market (+4)
5 Sell your horse (+5)
6 Steal a purse in the market (+6)
7 Buy an apprenticeship with a goldsmith (−7)
8 Win money in a game of dice (+8)
9 Win an archery contest (0)
10 Steal food from the market (+10)
11 Move into the goldsmith's house (0)
12 Kill a man in a fight (0)
13 Complete one year's work with no pay (−13)
14 Form a gang of outlaws (0)
15 Risk
16 Go to church regularly (0)
17 Give money to the poor (−17)
18 Risk

At the end of the game your teacher will collect the results and announce the winner. Then you have two pieces of written work to do.

1 Explain your progress in the game. Compare it with the winner's progress.
2 Write an illustrated diary about your life in a medieval town, describing all the moves you made in the game.

Apprentices 2

You should have found in the last game that it was a great advantage to sign up as an apprentice. Apprentices were usually boys aged 14 to 15 who signed on with a master craftsman for a period of 7, 9, 11 or 14 years. After this time, the apprentice would become a fully skilled craftsman and also a citizen of the town where he had served his apprenticeship.

The apprentice lived and worked with his master. Often rich tradesmen would have 10 or 12 working together and living in several rooms. The apprentices did not receive wages, but their meals and rooms were provided free and they also received instructions in their chosen trade and some general education.

An apprentice's family had to pay a lot of money to secure a place in a workshop. The master made rules which laid down the hours and conditions of work; the progress expected of the apprentice; and how he should behave. Apprentices were told to avoid gambling, strong drink and idleness. The guilds made certain that these apprenticeship rules were kept, since they did not want unskilled or foreign craftsmen trying to move in on the trades of the town.

Life was very hard for apprentices, but after they had finished their training they would be skilled craftsmen. Some of them grew rich and some became aldermen.

Dyers at work

Builders at work

The next exercise concentrates on the work done by apprentices. The picture opposite shows a *skinner's workshop*. The trade of skinning was an important one. Animal skins were carefully treated and tanned before being sold to clothiers and tailors who used them to make cloaks, breeches and boots. The skins were stretched and scraped, then treated with a mixture of alum (a chemical) and salt to dry the fat.

Four people are drawn in the workshop, but you cannot see what jobs they are doing. Underneath the picture the table explains the four most important jobs in a skinner's workshop. Study the information carefully.

1 Which jobs might each of the four people do?

2 Why did apprentices accept the jobs they were given?

3 What were the main disadvantages of being an apprentice?

4 Why was it an advantage for a master craftsman to take on several apprentices?

5 Write a paragraph explaining how a craft like skinning depended on a variety of skills and workers.

The Skinner's Workshop

Jobs

1 SCRAPING	2 TANNING	3 TRIMMING	4 SEWING
Scraping lumps of fat from the inside of untreated skins. Hard, dirty, smelly work. The skins are very large and awkward to handle. Plenty of blood and fleas and other insects.	Mixing tanning ingredients, soaking the skins in large vats and then treading them for five hours. Skins then dried and cleaned with chalk.	Tanned skins are dried further and inspected. Rough edges are cut off, holes repaired and the skins washed.	Trimmed pieces are sewn together to make one large skin. The pieces are carefully matched so that the final skin is strong and presentable.

Entertainments

Another important job for the aldermen and guilds was to organise entertainments for the citizens. These took place on feast days, saints' days or other holy days.

All apprentices were given the day off and there was a parade through the streets. Sports were played in the fields outside the town, giving the young men a chance to show off their bravery and skill.

Imagine you are a citizen of Maintown and a member of the Bakers' Guild. The town is going to organise a special celebration on Midsummer Day. The aim will be to attract visitors; to show off the trades of the town (leather and metal goods); and to celebrate the town's new charter and the building of a new church.

The town can only afford *one* of the events shown on the following pages. Read the information carefully, then write a letter to the aldermen saying which event would be best, giving as many reasons as possible for your choice.

The class, working in groups, will draw up a detailed programme showing how they would organise the Maintown Festival.

Event A: Chasing the Ball

Two teams of apprentices will be selected. There will be 30 boys in each team. The two sides will chase the ball (a pig's bladder) through the streets of the town, across the bridge and into the fields. There will be no rules. The many fights and disturbances will involve lots of spectators. Free beer will be provided for all those involved in the match.

Event B: A Mystery Play

A group of mummers (actors) will be invited from London. They will perform on a stage in the market-place and act out the story of Jesus, without speaking. The play will last all day—sunrise to sunset—and at noon there will be a break when food will be served. The costumes and stage will be made by local craftsmen and apprentices.

A mystery play

Event C: Blood Sports

There will be three main items, taking place in the fields:

1 Cock-fighting: two trained cocks will fight each other.
2 Bear-baiting: a savage brown bear will be tied to a pole and left to defend itself against a pack of 15 dogs until it is killed.
3 Hare-coursing: hares will be chased by dogs over a marked course.

These events should attract many spectators and bring in a lot of money.

'Of the Sports of London': William FitzStephen (1170)

Every year on the day called Carnival, scholars from the different schools bring fighting cocks. The whole day is a holiday to watch cock-fighting. After dinner, the young men go into the suburbs to play ball.

Every Sunday in Lent after dinner a fresh swarm of young men goes forth into the fields on war-horses. They fight each other, while others carry spears (with the point removed) and fight on foot. At Easter, they play at a kind of naval warfare. A shield is tied firmly to a tree in mid-stream, and a small boat carries on the stern a youth armed with a lance. He aims to hit the shield and break the lance, without falling into the river. On feast days throughout the summer the young men take part in the sports of archery, running, jumping, wrestling, slinging the stone, throwing the javelin and fighting with swords.

In winter of every feast day, boars, armed with strong tusks, fight for their lives 'to save their bacon', or huge bears do battle with the dogs let loose on them. When the marsh is frozen over, swarms of young men run to play games on the ice. Some make seats out of a large lump of ice, and whilst one sits thereon, others with linked hands run before and drag him along behind them. Others put on their feet the shin-bones of animals, binding them firmly round their ankles, and holding poles in their hands which they strike from time to time against the ice, they are propelled swift as a bird.

1 List the sports played in London in 1170. How many are still played today?

2 Which of the following groups would, or would not, enjoy feast days? Explain your answers.
(a) Apprentices
(b) Housewives
(c) Criminals
(d) Priests

3 Explain where the word 'holiday' comes from.

4 Give an example of
(a) a blood sport involving animals, (b) a sport that was useful for training fighters.

5 Look carefully at the pictures of medieval people that you have seen in this section. Suggest what a 'cutpurse' might have done for a living. Draw a series of pictures to show clearly how he went about his trade.

---

6 Use what you have learnt to complete the word puzzle below. Make your own copy of the puzzle.

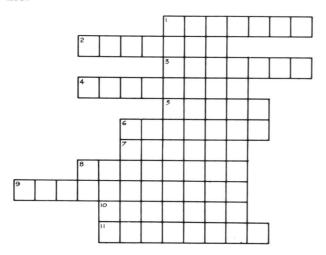

DOWN
1 A sport with dogs and another 4-legged animal (2 words)

ACROSS
1 A medieval football
2 Actors who never spoke
3 A war sport
4 A guild officer
5 Much of this was spilt in medieval sports
6 One of the major products of Maintown
7 ....days were a good excuse for a celebration
8 Documents signed by the King which allowed towns to hold fairs
9 Trainee craftsmen
10 The flags of the guilds which were paraded through the streets
11 Entertainers with skilful hands

The Village

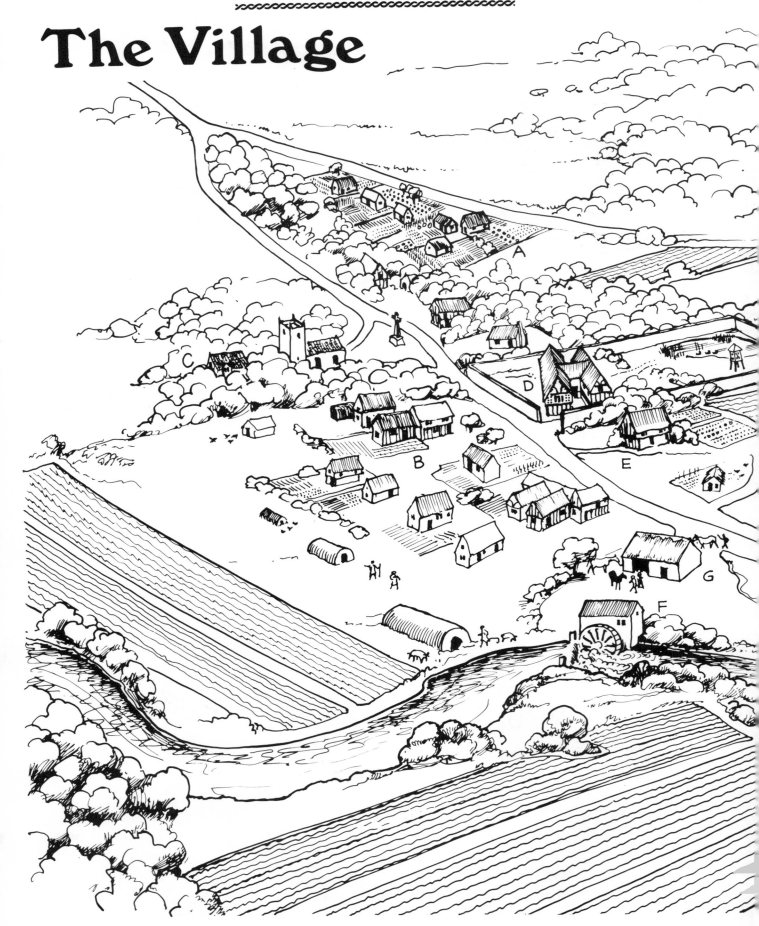

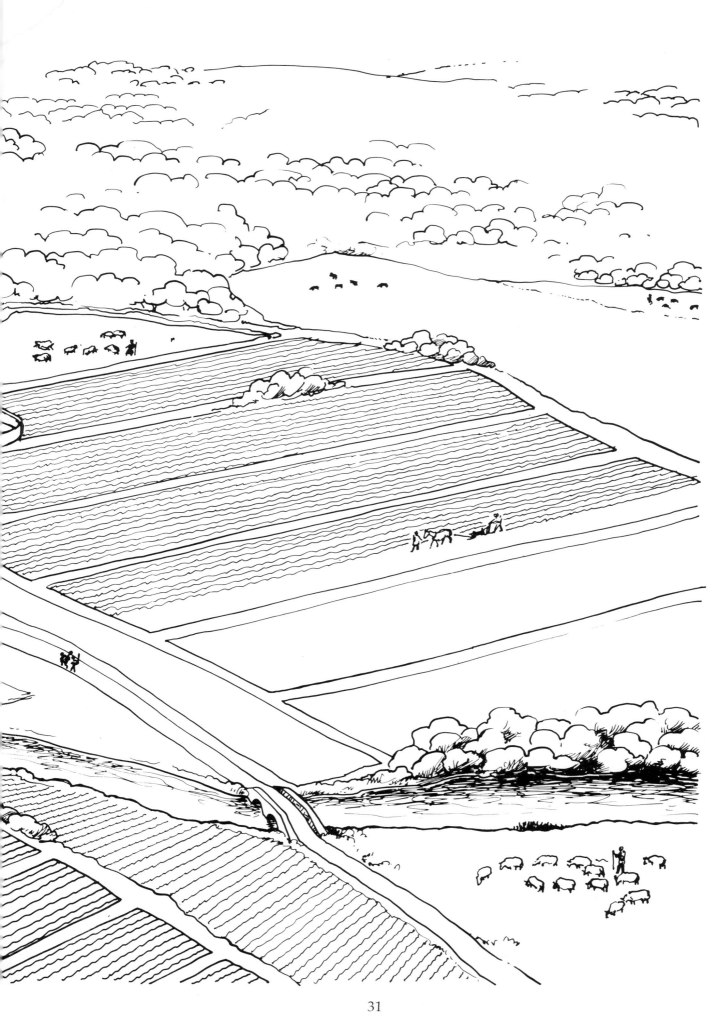

People of the Village

The Priest
He is in charge of the local church. He holds services and reads prayers. He also looks after the sick and poor people of the village. He spends some time helping on the land.

The Reeve
He reports to the bailiff and receives instructions about farm work. He has to make sure that the villeins carry out their duties properly. He is himself a villein who has been chosen for this job by the bailiff or the lord.

The Cottar
Cottars only had a small piece of land—usually the garden surrounding their houses. They were the poorest people in the village and often had to beg or steal to get enough to eat.

The drawing on pages 30 and 31 shows a typical English village in 1300. Notice the very large fields surrounding the village, the small huts, the church and the large manor house.

Villager	House	Reason
1		
2		
3		
4		
5		
6		

Make a table like the one above. Look carefully at the picture of the village and at the descriptions under the pictures of the villagers.

1 Put the villagers into the table in order of their rank, the most important first.

2 Find the five houses marked on the picture. On the table show where each of the villagers lived. Notice two of them live in the same house. (The houses are labelled A to E.)

3 Write a sentence on each of the six village characters explaining why you chose that particular house for him or her.

4 Compare the houses and land farmed by a villein and a cottar. Which person would be thought to be more important in the village?

5 Explain the jobs done by the bailiff and the reeve. What sort of person would make a good bailiff?

6 Find the water mill (F). What do you think it was used for? How else can a mill be powered?

7 Find the smithy (G). Make a list of things a smith could make that would be useful to the villagers.

Lord of the Manor
A very rich and powerful nobleman. Like many other noblemen he is related to the King. He owns manors in southern England. He is expected to travel around the country with the King's court and he has fought in France with the King.

The Bailiff
A sensible, hard-working man appointed by the lord to look after his manor (all the land owned by the lord). He is in charge of the farming, the crops and all the villagers. He is given money, land and clothes by the lord of the manor. He lives in the lord's house.

The Villein
Most men of the village are villeins. They are farm workers who are allowed to work the land in the large fields. They cannot move to the town. They work for the lord, pay taxes, harvest crops, build houses and keep the village going.

The Reeve at Work

1 Why does the reeve wear a horn?

2 Name two jobs the reeve would supervise.

3 What evidence is there in this picture that the reeve thought he was better than the other villagers?

4 Why might the reeve be an unpopular man in the village?

5 What sort of person would be likely to make a good reeve?

The Farming Year

On pages 36 and 37 there is a board game about the villein's year in the village.

> **Rules**
>
> **1** Toss a coin to move: heads—move two circles; tails—move one circle.
>
> **2** Use some suitable token to show where you are on the board—perhaps a coin, a drawing pin or a small piece of paper. You could make some interesting counters shaped like medieval farm tools.
>
> **3** Make a note of the things that happen to you during the game (using *only* the circles on which you land).

Sowing

Reaping

Collecting corn

When you have finished the game, use your list of happenings to write a diary of the year in your life in a medieval village. You can make this even more interesting by drawing some of the events and doing extra research to add to your own details. Remember, this is what has happened to *you,* so describe your feelings as you go along. Ask your teacher to explain any strange words in the game.

Answer these questions:

1 Why did the villeins often get annoyed with the reeve?

2 Which season brought the hardest work? Explain why this was so.

3 Which was the most uncomfortable season for the villein? Explain why.

4 Why did many villeins go poaching?

5 What do you think '*dry* boon work' was?

6 What payments did the villein have to make during the year? Why do you think he had to make these payments? How do you think he paid?

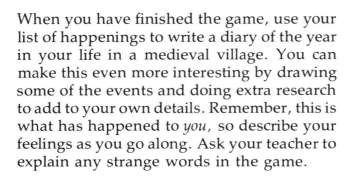

The Plough

Ploughing was one of the most important jobs for the villeins and ploughmen. Ploughing breaks up the soil so that crops can be planted. It is done every year and sometimes twice a year. The picture on page 34 shows a typical plough of the time.

To find out how a plough works follow these instructions:

1 Trace the pieces of the plough shown below accurately onto a sheet of paper.

2 Cut the pieces out. You should cut along the dotted lines as if they were solid.

3 Assemble the pieces of the plough from the following information:

(a) The main part of the plough (3) is placed in the middle of your page.

(b) (1) is a *handle* to which other pieces are fastened.

(c) The *coulter* (4) was a blade which cut the ground at the front of the plough.

(d) The *ploughshare* (5) was a pointed blade which cut the furrow and turned the soil. It was partly hidden by the *mouldboard*.

(e) The *mouldboard* (2) was at the back of the plough. The earth slid over it and fell in a heap at the side of the plough.

4 When you have checked with your teacher and looked at the picture on page 34, stick the plough together.

5 You can put it in the centre of your page and draw a farming scene around it. Colour in the plough using different colours for the metal and wooden parts.

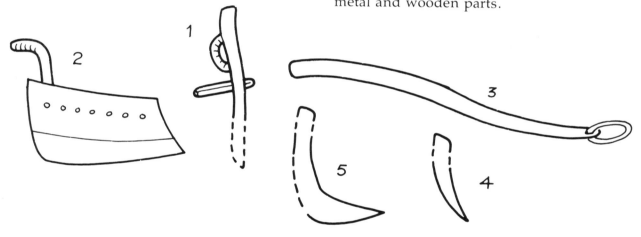

(Look at the picture on the left to help you with some of the answers.)

1 Which animals are being used to pull the plough?

2 Medieval pictures often show two men behind the plough. Suggest reasons for this.

3 What was the job done by the person walking beside the plough?

4 Can you suggest any simple additions to the plough shown which could make it easier to use?

5 Explain with diagrams how the plough cuts the soil and piles it in ridges.

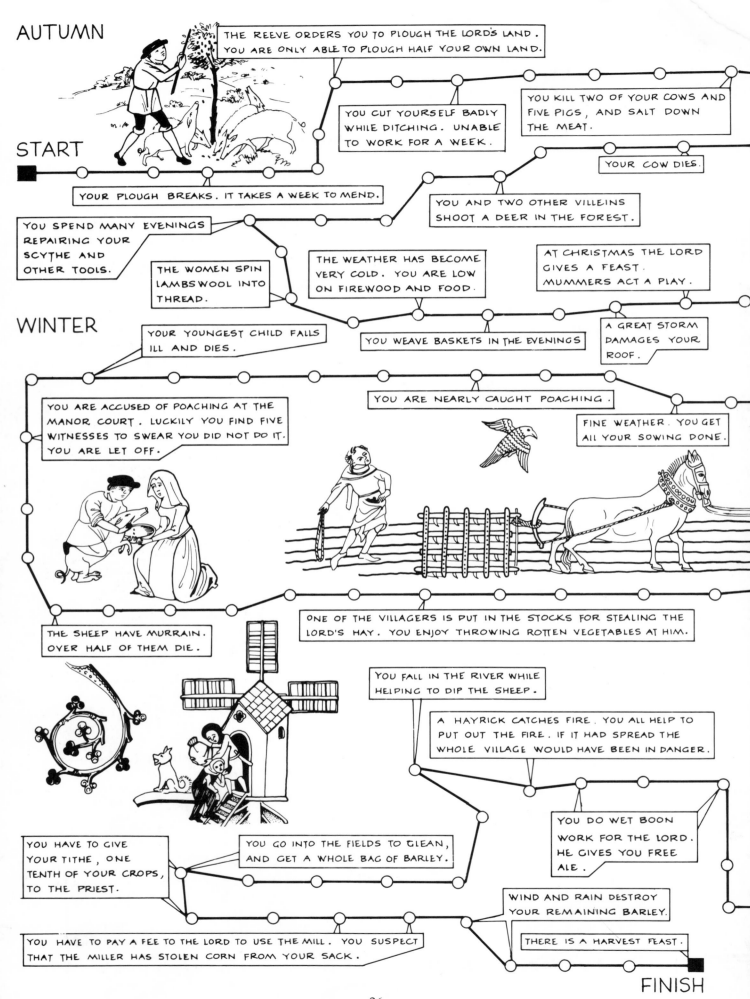

AUTUMN

THE REEVE ORDERS YOU TO PLOUGH THE LORD'S LAND. YOU ARE ONLY ABLE TO PLOUGH HALF YOUR OWN LAND.

START

YOU CUT YOURSELF BADLY WHILE DITCHING. UNABLE TO WORK FOR A WEEK.

YOU KILL TWO OF YOUR COWS AND FIVE PIGS, AND SALT DOWN THE MEAT.

YOUR COW DIES.

YOUR PLOUGH BREAKS. IT TAKES A WEEK TO MEND.

YOU AND TWO OTHER VILLEINS SHOOT A DEER IN THE FOREST.

YOU SPEND MANY EVENINGS REPAIRING YOUR SCYTHE AND OTHER TOOLS.

THE WOMEN SPIN LAMBSWOOL INTO THREAD.

THE WEATHER HAS BECOME VERY COLD. YOU ARE LOW ON FIREWOOD AND FOOD.

AT CHRISTMAS THE LORD GIVES A FEAST. MUMMERS ACT A PLAY.

WINTER

YOUR YOUNGEST CHILD FALLS ILL AND DIES.

YOU WEAVE BASKETS IN THE EVENINGS

A GREAT STORM DAMAGES YOUR ROOF.

YOU ARE ACCUSED OF POACHING AT THE MANOR COURT. LUCKILY YOU FIND FIVE WITNESSES TO SWEAR YOU DID NOT DO IT. YOU ARE LET OFF.

YOU ARE NEARLY CAUGHT POACHING.

FINE WEATHER. YOU GET ALL YOUR SOWING DONE.

THE SHEEP HAVE MURRAIN. OVER HALF OF THEM DIE.

ONE OF THE VILLAGERS IS PUT IN THE STOCKS FOR STEALING THE LORD'S HAY. YOU ENJOY THROWING ROTTEN VEGETABLES AT HIM.

YOU FALL IN THE RIVER WHILE HELPING TO DIP THE SHEEP.

A HAYRICK CATCHES FIRE. YOU ALL HELP TO PUT OUT THE FIRE. IF IT HAD SPREAD THE WHOLE VILLAGE WOULD HAVE BEEN IN DANGER.

YOU DO WET BOON WORK FOR THE LORD. HE GIVES YOU FREE ALE.

YOU HAVE TO GIVE YOUR TITHE, ONE TENTH OF YOUR CROPS, TO THE PRIEST.

YOU GO INTO THE FIELDS TO GLEAN, AND GET A WHOLE BAG OF BARLEY.

WIND AND RAIN DESTROY YOUR REMAINING BARLEY.

YOU HAVE TO PAY A FEE TO THE LORD TO USE THE MILL. YOU SUSPECT THAT THE MILLER HAS STOLEN CORN FROM YOUR SACK.

THERE IS A HARVEST FEAST.

FINISH

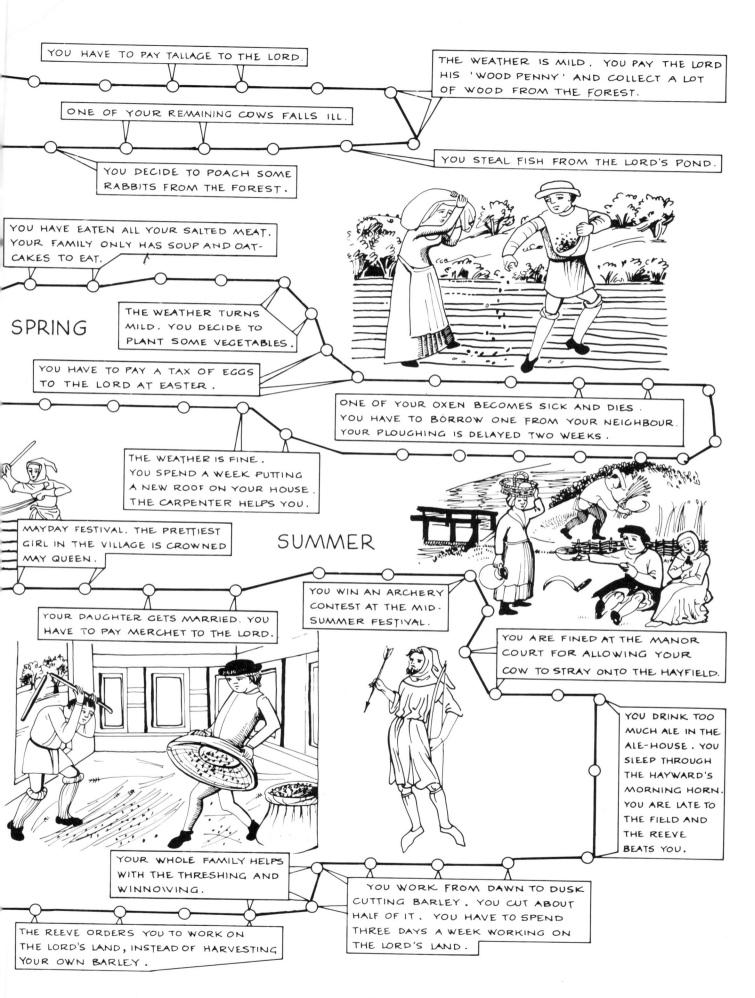

YOU HAVE TO PAY TALLAGE TO THE LORD.

THE WEATHER IS MILD. YOU PAY THE LORD HIS 'WOOD PENNY' AND COLLECT A LOT OF WOOD FROM THE FOREST.

ONE OF YOUR REMAINING COWS FALLS ILL.

YOU STEAL FISH FROM THE LORD'S POND.

YOU DECIDE TO POACH SOME RABBITS FROM THE FOREST.

YOU HAVE EATEN ALL YOUR SALTED MEAT. YOUR FAMILY ONLY HAS SOUP AND OAT-CAKES TO EAT.

SPRING

THE WEATHER TURNS MILD. YOU DECIDE TO PLANT SOME VEGETABLES.

YOU HAVE TO PAY A TAX OF EGGS TO THE LORD AT EASTER.

ONE OF YOUR OXEN BECOMES SICK AND DIES. YOU HAVE TO BORROW ONE FROM YOUR NEIGHBOUR. YOUR PLOUGHING IS DELAYED TWO WEEKS.

THE WEATHER IS FINE. YOU SPEND A WEEK PUTTING A NEW ROOF ON YOUR HOUSE. THE CARPENTER HELPS YOU.

MAYDAY FESTIVAL. THE PRETTIEST GIRL IN THE VILLAGE IS CROWNED MAY QUEEN.

SUMMER

YOU WIN AN ARCHERY CONTEST AT THE MID-SUMMER FESTIVAL.

YOUR DAUGHTER GETS MARRIED. YOU HAVE TO PAY MERCHET TO THE LORD.

YOU ARE FINED AT THE MANOR COURT FOR ALLOWING YOUR COW TO STRAY ONTO THE HAYFIELD.

YOU DRINK TOO MUCH ALE IN THE ALE-HOUSE. YOU SLEEP THROUGH THE HAYWARD'S MORNING HORN. YOU ARE LATE TO THE FIELD AND THE REEVE BEATS YOU.

YOUR WHOLE FAMILY HELPS WITH THE THRESHING AND WINNOWING.

YOU WORK FROM DAWN TO DUSK CUTTING BARLEY. YOU CUT ABOUT HALF OF IT. YOU HAVE TO SPEND THREE DAYS A WEEK WORKING ON THE LORD'S LAND.

THE REEVE ORDERS YOU TO WORK ON THE LORD'S LAND, INSTEAD OF HARVESTING YOUR OWN BARLEY.

Designing an Open Field

Ridges and furrows can still be seen from the air

gore —

headland —

— land

ridge

furrow

The main unit of ploughed earth was the 'land'. This was as much as an ox team could plough in one morning. Each land was about 200 metres long and 20 metres wide (about 1 acre). It was rectangular in shape.

As many lands as possible were fitted into one field. The part left over round the edges, where there was not enough room for a whole land and where the plough had to turn, was called the headland.

Any awkward shapes remaining were ploughed as well as possible. They were called gores. Very little land was left unploughed in a field.

Each ploughed area had to have a path round it so that the villagers could move around without damaging the crops.

Each villein was given two or three furrows in a number of lands, headlands and gores in the three fields which surrounded the village. In this way the good and bad land was shared out fairly among the villagers.

Each villein would have a total of two lands (although this was made up of furrows in many different places) and he could keep the crops grown on his furrows.

The lord of the manor had about one-third of the lands. His furrows were also scattered and the villeins had to farm his land for him.

You can design your own medieval open field in any or all of the following ways:

1 Copy or trace the field pattern on page 39. Show the direction of the furrows and label each piece Land, Headland or Gore. Colour in the paths.

2 Copy or trace the field pattern on page 39. Cut out pieces of paper to match the lands, headlands and gores. Draw and colour on them the furrows and stick them onto your field pattern to make the patchwork of ploughed land.

3 Draw your own field pattern to scale (after looking at the example on page 39) and design your own lands, headlands and gores to fit.

4 Divide into groups. Design your own field patterns for the three fields around the village. Draw them on large sheets of paper or card for a class exhibition. When you have done this, colour in the furrows of one villein and the lord. Use different colours for each and make a key. If you work as a group you could do the strips of a number of villeins and draw the village as well. Colour the houses in the same way as the strips to show where the villeins live.

The Field Pattern

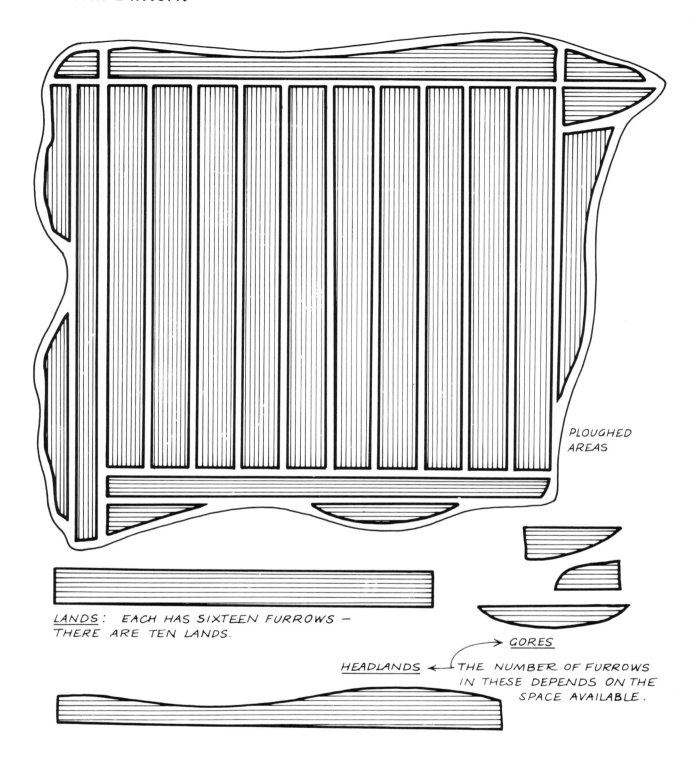

PLOUGHED
AREAS

LANDS: EACH HAS SIXTEEN FURROWS —
THERE ARE TEN LANDS.

GORES

HEADLANDS ← THE NUMBER OF FURROWS
IN THESE DEPENDS ON THE
SPACE AVAILABLE.

1 Why was a land a morning's ploughing? Why was it not bigger?

2 How many mornings would it take the villagers to plough this whole field?

3 What disadvantages were there for a villein in having his furrows widely scattered?

4 What advantages were there for the villein?

5 Just by looking at the field pattern shown can you think of any ways in which hard-working villeins could be rewarded, and lazy villeins punished?

6 Why was a well-designed field pattern vital for the village?

7 When you have done the work 'Designing an Open Field' calculate the area of farmland around the village in the picture on pages 30 and 31.

Will the Villein

Will has lived in the village all his life. He is now 30 years old. He is married with two children (boys aged 8 and 10). He farms 26 furrows of land which are scattered about the three fields.

He built his house himself with timber, mud and straw, although he needed help from his friend, Tom the Thatcher, to get the roof right.

He owns two oxen, four chickens, a horse and three sheep which graze on the common. He usually grows rye on his land. He takes the rye to the mill to be ground into flour, which his wife bakes into loaves of hard, dry bread. Will says this bread keeps longer than fancy white bread and fills his stomach better.

Will spends three days a week working on Lord Hazlemere's land. He is a strong, healthy man who is popular with the reeve and bailiff. Will owns nothing else. He has never left the village and he has never learnt to read, write or tackle a skilled job.

The Problems of the Peasants
(adapted from *Piers Plowman*)

The poorest people are our neighbours, if we notice right well,
Like prisoners in dungeons are the poor folk in cottages.
Burdened by their children and their lord's rent
What they save by spinning they spend on house hire [rent],
Or in milk and meal to make porridge
To cheer up their children who cry for their food.
And they themselves suffer surely much hunger
And trouble in the winter, with waking at nights
And rising to rock their restless babies,
Carding and combing, mending and washing,
Rubbing and winding wool. They have rushes to peel.*
So we must not hide the truth about
The problems of these women
And of many men who suffer much unhappiness.
Crippled with hunger and thirst, they keep up appearances
And would be ashamed to beg.

To peel rushes: to make rush lights.

1 Make a list of all the things that Will owns. Was he a rich man?

2 Explain why Will could not do the following jobs without help from the other villeins:
(a) ploughing his land
(b) bringing in the harvest
(c) looking after his animals every day

3 Will was not a free man. He had to work for Lord Hazlemere and would be punished if he tried to run away or avoid work. Can you think of any other possible reasons why Will stayed in the village?

4 Explain why Will needs help from the four men described below, who also live in the village.

JOHN THE BLACKSMITH
He makes all the iron tools in the village. He makes ploughshares and mend ploughs. He makes horseshoes. He also makes iron pots for cooking.

TOM THE THATCHER
He cuts the reeds from the river. He cuts twigs and branches from the forest. He places these in bundles and dries them out. These materials are then used to thatch the roofs of houses, huts and barns. He also thatches the tops of haystacks.

WILFRED THE CARPENTER
He has the tools and the skill to make wooden boxes, chairs and tables. He repairs ploughs. He makes the yokes for the oxen. He also helps in building. He does all the detailed and difficult work that the villagers cannot do themselves.

MARK THE MILLER
He runs the mill which is owned by the lord. The villagers are not allowed to own their own mill-stones. They bring their corn to him to be ground into flour. Mark is not very popular as the villagers suspect him of stealing from their sacks.

The Manor Court

The lord of the manor was often a great nobleman or church leader. He owned the land in many villages. Not only did the villagers work for him, they also had to pay regular fines—payments of money or goods.

For instance, a villager would have to pay an *entry fine* when first building a cottage. A fine

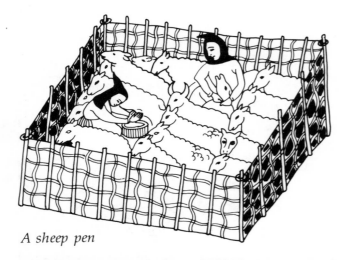

A sheep pen

had to be paid when someone married. The villagers paid fines for cutting timber and quarrying stone. They also had to provide meat, eggs and wheat as an Easter gift for the lord. This was because all the land belonged to the lord.

Finally, the villagers were expected to look after their own cottages properly and also the large barns, sheep pens and other buildings belonging to the lord. If the village was not kept in good repair, all the villagers would have to pay a *penalty* to the lord. This could be quite a large sum of money.

The reeve and the bailiff would check that all these rules were being obeyed. They held regular meetings in the manor house, at which the villagers were told about fines and payments. These meetings were known as *Manor Courts*. Many lords kept records of these courts. These records were known as Manor Rolls.

The following extracts are taken from the Manor Rolls of the Prior of Durham, written in 1378. The Prior was a great churchman who owned many villages in Northumberland. Read the extracts, then answer the questions.

Village of Billingham

1 Alice Waus had to pay a fine of 6 pence in order to get married.

2 All the villagers were to repair the sheep-pen before the next manor court, or pay a penalty of 40 shillings.

3 All the villagers were ordered to keep off the path across the land called Litilmeres in the holding of Henry of Neuraw, on the penalty of 12 pence.

4 It was ordered that everyone should help to look after the pigs and that every one of them should guard them when his turn came . . . on penalty of 12 pence.

5 It was ordered that none of the villagers should dig in the high street of the village of Billingham, on pain of 40 pence.

Village of Ferryhill

1 All the tenants of the village were ordered that none of them should play football on penalty of paying 40 shillings.

2 William Adlok took 20 acres of land last held by Thomas Gawd . . . gersum (entry fine) of 10 shillings to be paid.

1 Why did Alice Waus and William Adlok have to pay fines?

2 What was an entry fine? Who paid it and who got the money?

3 Why might all the villagers in Ferryhill and Billingham have to pay 40 shillings?

4 Why did Henry of Neuraw like the decision of the Manor Court?

5 What advantages did (a) the lord, and (b) the villagers get from the meeting of the Manor Courts?

The behaviour of the villeins was also judged at the Manor Court. The reeve and the bailiff would point out villeins who had been lazy, or anyone who had been caught stealing, and any person who had failed to keep to the customs of the village.

The customs were a set of rules which explained the relationship between lord and villagers. They were sometimes written down, but often not. People who had broken the customs would be called to give an account of themselves. If they were found guilty they would be fined or made to work extra hours.

Customs of the Village

1 Each villein shall pay the same annual tallage (tax) to the lord.

2 Each villein shall give the lord 12 eggs at Easter, or their value.

3 On the marriage of his daughter, a villein shall pay a fine to the lord.

4 A fine must be paid by a villein if his son leaves the village.

5 On the death of his father, a villein shall give his best animal to the lord of the manor.

6 Each villein shall be liable to week work (on the lord's land) on Mondays, Tuesdays, Thursdays and Saturdays.

7 Each villein shall provide an additional 12 days per year as boon work.

8 No villein shall let his animals graze on the lord's land.

9 Each villein shall give one-tenth of his produce (wheat or barley or other crops) to the Church.

10 No hut shall be built on cultivated land.

11 An entry fine shall be paid by any villein who wishes to take over his father's land.

12 The lake, wood, and pastures are to be owned by the lord.

13 Each villein may take one cartload of wood for his own use, but no animals or fish from the village.

14 No land can be exchanged or sold.

15 No villein may leave the village.

16 Flour must be made in the village mill and a fine must be paid to the miller for the use of the mill.

17 The cottars have no grazing rights, and no right to wood or animals.

The Reeve Reports

Imagine you are the reeve of a medieval village. On Monday 1st August you kept an eye on 5 villagers. You noted how they spent their day. Study the customs of the village (above) and the notes about what the villagers did (page 44). Prepare a case against any or all of the people you feel have broken the village customs. Remember the more people you can catch, the bigger your reputation will be.

You could work in a number of ways:

1 Reports. You can write your cases in the form of reports. You should include an account of the person's day and comment on his or her general attitude and performance.

2 Extra customs. You could work in groups and make up some sensible extra customs for the village.

3 Drama. You could invent some custom-breakers of your own and then make up a play about what they did, how they were caught and what they said in the Manor Court.

4 Role play. Your teacher could make up a role and then you could interview him (or her) to find out what he (or she) did during the day, and whether he (or she) has broken any of the village customs.

The Reeve's Notes on the Villagers' Movements on 1st August

1 Will (villein)

He got out of bed at dawn (6 a.m.) when you called the villagers to work. He spent 4 hours working in the fields, cutting corn, then another 4 hours bringing corn into the manor storage barn. In the evening he helped the blacksmith with his work and repaired his own hut.

2 Ralf (villein)

He got out of bed at about 9 a.m., when you sent your boy to fetch him. He spent an hour working in the fields, cutting corn, and then another 4 hours bringing corn into the manor storage barn. In the evening, he collected 2 cartloads of wood from the forest, and spent some time working in his hut.

3 Alice (cottar)

She got up at dawn and helped with threshing the corn. Then she spent several hours working in her garden. She was called to drive her 2 pigs from the north field before supper. She ate a meal of rye bread and soup, and then went collecting firewood.

4 Hugh (villein)

He got out of bed before dawn and was waiting for you as you went round the village. He spent 4 hours working in the fields, cutting corn, and another 2 hours bringing corn into the manor barn. He then spent some time asleep in the field. In the evening he was seen fishing in the village stream.

5 Rob (villein)

He got out of bed at dawn and went straight to the fields. He spent 4 hours working there. After this he spent 4 hours in the manor barn, then he went to the miller to grind some rye. He paid the miller 1 penny. He took 4 sacks of flour to the churchyard. He then set out to look for his son who ran away to the town 3 weeks ago and has not returned.

Here are three activities to help you test your knowledge of medieval country life.

1 Complete the word puzzle. All the words are farming activities and end in -ing.

DOWN

1 Using a horse-drawn rake

ACROSS

1 Gathering the crops
2 Stealing the lord's animals
3 Keeping food for winter
4 Cutting wool
5 Preparing land for seed
6 Planting
7 Weeding
8 Grinding corn into flour
9 Picking up all the grains of corn that have been dropped in the fields

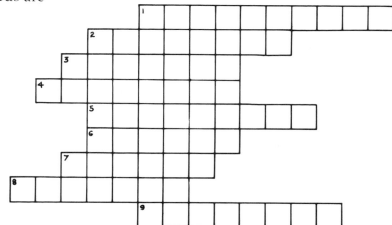

2 Make a table like this (yours will be bigger) and fill it in with activities which went on in each season. There is a list below to help you. You can put in the answers from the word puzzle and any others you can remember.
You can use pictures if you prefer.

List of activities

Finding firewood	Slaughtering	Milking
Repairing houses	Lambing	Egg collecting
Making tools	Paying taxes to	Bird scaring
Threshing	the lord	Muck spreading
Winnowing	Building	Boon work

AUTUMN	WINTER
SPRING	SUMMER

3

Who is the man leaning on his stick? What is his job?

Who owns the large house in the background?

Who would be likely to own the smaller house?

Explain what each of the people shown in the picture is doing.

Work in a village

45

The Parish Church....

How the Church Was Organised in the Middle Ages

At the head
THE POPE

He was the representative of God on Earth. He was very powerful and everyone obeyed him.

below him
ARCHBISHOPS AND BISHOPS

They were often rich and powerful. They owned a lot of land. They spent much time advising the King.

at the bottom
THE PARISH PRIESTS

They were very poor and did most of the hard work.

Why the Church Was So Important in the Middle Ages

Reason 1

People believed very strongly in Heaven and Hell. People who lived wicked lives would be sent to Hell when they died. They would stay there for ever and be horribly punished for their sins. People who were good would go to Heaven and live in perfect happiness. The only way to Heaven was through the Church.

Reason 2

Life in the Middle Ages was very tough. There was much disease, poverty and misery. The parish priests gave simple, practical help to those in need. You will read more about this on page 47.

You will read more about this on page 47.

Reason 3

The parish church was the centre of village life. People went to church almost every day. Apart from the services, villagers went there to talk, pick up the latest news and gossip, have lessons from the priest and even hold markets, festivals and games.

The village of Biddenden in Kent

Plan of the village

.... and Parish Priests

The parish priests were very poor. Many were unable to read or write. They had to learn the Latin services off by heart. They were often unpaid. They spent a lot of time working in the fields, just like the villagers. There was a special piece of land put aside for them, called the Glebe.

The Job

Apart from giving the services the priest would hear confessions and give forgiveness to people who were sorry for their sins. He was expected to keep the church in good repair. He visited the sick; comforted people in times of trouble; and gave shelter, food and clothing to the poor.

The priest performed the three most important ceremonies of a villager's life—christening, marriage and burial. When people were dying they would send for the priest and he would give them the 'last rites'—he heard them confess all their sins and gave them forgiveness.

Tithes

The villagers had to give a tithe (tenth) of what they produced to the Church. This would be stored in a tithe barn until it was collected and taken away by Church officials. Very little was given to the priest.

The villagers were usually glad to help the priest by providing money, labour and goods to keep the church going.

1 Copy the plan of the village opposite. Colour in the church and churchyard. Make a list of the things that went on in or near the church.

2 Which is the largest building in the village?

3 Look at the picture of the parish priest. Describe what he looks like. Explain what he is carrying and why he is carrying them.

4 Why were bishops and archbishops so rich?

5 Write an advertisement for a parish priest. Explain what sort of man should apply for the job and what he will be expected to do.

6 Why were the last rites so important to people in the Middle Ages?

7 Why did so many people go to church in the Middle Ages?

8 Here are 3 households in the Middle Ages. Explain, in each case, what help the parish priest could give them.

(a) A family of 5—a mother and 4 young children. The father, a villein, has just died. The family has no money. They are starving and badly need clothes for the winter.

(b) A family of 8. The father, a ploughman, has just broken his leg. He is in great pain and will not be able to work for several months. His wife is very depressed. One of the children is ill.

(c) An old man who is dying, and his wife. He is worried that she will starve when he dies. He is also worried about all the sins he has committed in his life.

Monks and Monasteries

There was a great increase in the number of monks and monasteries during the Middle Ages. Monks were dedicated men who gave up everything to join a monastery. They were not allowed to marry, to wear fine clothes, or to eat and drink too much.

They spent their time praying and working inside the monastery. They believed that they were leading the perfect Christian life and so would be guaranteed a place in Heaven. They offered prayers not only for themselves, but also for other people outside the monastery.

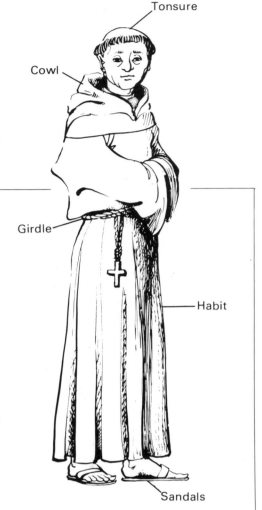

Tonsure
The hair was cut like this to represent the 'crown of thorns' worn by Christ when he was crucified.

Cowl
This was a hood.

Girdle
The monks wore a simple belt to show that they still belonged to the world. On it hung the cross, the symbol of being a monk.

Habit
The monks wore the simplest robe they could. It was made of rough cloth so that it would irritate their skin and remind them all the time of the suffering of Christ.

Sandals
These simple shoes reminded the monks that they had to be humble like Christ.

1 Draw a picture of the monk.

2 Describe what monks wore. Why did they wear simple clothes?

3 Name the largest building in the monastery.

4 Explain what you think was the most important activity for monks.

5 Describe what the monks did in each of the buildings marked on the picture of the monastery. Say why each was important for the monastery.

6 Why is the monastery in the country and not in the town?

Monks at work

A Medieval Monastery

*Fountains Abbey in Yorkshire
as it is today*

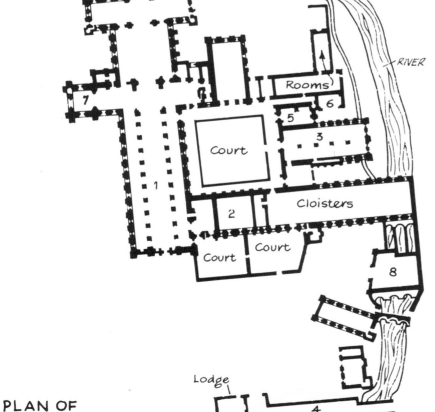

**PLAN OF
FOUNTAINS ABBEY**

1 CHURCH
2 DORMITORY
3 REFECTORY
4 INFIRMARY
5 KITCHEN
6 WASH-HOUSE
7 TOWER
8 CHAPEL. THE
   POOR WERE
   FED HERE DAILY

Monastery Life

The Rule of St Benedict was the basic code of conduct for all monks in the Early Middle Ages. Here are some extracts from the Rule.

1 No one should do what he wants . . . or argue with the Abbot.

2 The brothers [monks] shall take turns to wait on one another so that no one is excused from kitchen work.

3 At brothers' mealtimes there should always be a Bible reading . . . There shall be complete silence at table and no whispering.

4 The brothers should pass to each other in turn whatever food is needed . . . If anything should be wanted, ask for it by signs.

5 Above all, care must be taken of the sick.

6 As the prophet says 'Seven times in the day do I praise thee', so we will have seven church services a day.

7 Idleness is the enemy of the soul. Therefore, at fixed times, the brothers should be busy with manual work; and at other times with holy reading.

8 A mattress, woollen blanket and a pillow should be enough bedding.

Monk's Timetable

1.45 a.m.	Wake up. Private reading and prayer
2.00 a.m.	Church service
3.30 a.m.	Sleep (summer only)
4.00 a.m.	Church service
5.00 a.m.	Private reading and prayer
6.00 a.m.	Church service then eat
7.00 a.m.	Work
8.00 a.m.	Church service
9.15 a.m.	Work
11.45 a.m.	Church service
Midday	Meal
1.00 p.m.	Private reading and prayer
1.45 p.m.	Sleep (summer only)
2.45 p.m.	Church service
3.00 p.m.	Work
5.45 p.m.	Meal
6.00 p.m.	Church service
7.15 p.m.	Private reading and prayer
7.45 p.m.	Church service
8.00 p.m.	Bed

Look at each of the rules indicated and answer all the questions.

1 (Rule 1) Who was the leader of the monastery?

2 (Rule 2) Explain what the point of this rule is.

3 (Rule 3) What would be heard at meal times? What was the point of this rule?

4 (Rules 1, 3, 7, 8) What were some of the disadvantages of living in a monastery? If life was so uncomfortable, why did so many people want to join monasteries?

5 Why did monks work?

6 How could some monasteries become very rich?

7 Look carefully at the pictures to help you answer this question and think about the Rules and the reasons for them.
Here is a list of possible activities for monks. Arrange them into 2 columns headed: Likely activities for monks; Unlikely activities for monks.

Praying, Gardening, Keeping bees, Copying books by hand, Gambling, Learning to fight, Brewing strong liquor, Fishing, Fasting, Singing, Fish farming, Weaving, Mixing medicine, Baking, Riding, Begging, Going to towns, Looking after guests, Painting, Building, Carpentry, Keeping accounts, Dancing.

Choose 2 activities you have put into the 'unlikely' column and explain why you put them there.

Most monks spent several hours a day praying, singing and reading the Bible. They believed this would help others as well as themselves.

Monks worked both inside and outside the monastery. They produced all their own food, some of which they gave to the poor. Each monastery was like a village with its own craftsmen and workers.

The Friars

Monasteries soon grew to be rich and powerful in England. Rich men offered gifts of land and money. Many monasteries had large libraries and guest rooms where people could stay for nothing. Cistercian monks reclaimed huge areas of waste land, which they used for sheep farming. They sold wool in England or abroad. The abbot of a large monastery would often be a friend and adviser to the king. Although they still gave money to the poor, monks rather cut themselves off from local village life.

In the thirteenth century, the Franciscan friars arrived in England. They were followers of St Francis of Assisi, and they believed that the monks were not doing their job properly. They felt that the monks had forgotten that they should go about and teach people. The friars insisted on travelling from village to village. They held open-air services and helped people in need. The friars took great pride in being poor, but before long they began to receive gifts and began to build great houses rather like the monasteries. By 1282, there were 1,583 Franciscan houses in Europe.

A friar preaching

St Francis of Assisi (born 1181)

St Francis of Assisi helping a poor man

St Francis took a vow of poverty, promising never to own anything and to serve the Pope. 'Until now I have called Pietro Bernadone my father, but now that I intend to serve the Lord I am returning all the money and all the clothes that were his property.'

The Rules of St Francis

"This is the rule and way of life of the brothers minor: to observe the Holy Gospel of our Lord Jesus Christ, living in obedience, without personal possessions and in chastity. Brother Francis promises obedience and reverence to our Lord Pope Honorius, and to his successors and to the Roman Church."

Rules for Friars

1 Friars should not quarrel.
2 Friars should pray daily and do no work on Fridays and Holy Days.
3 Friars should not ride on horses unless they are sick.
4 A Friar's only clothes should be 2 gowns, a belt and a cape.
5 Friars should love their enemies.
6 Friars should always obey their leaders.
7 Friars must not own anything.
8 Friars should not accept money.
9 Friars should pass an examination before going out to preach.
10 Friars should never talk to women and should not visit nunneries.

Comparing Monks and Friars

The table below shows some of the jobs done by monks and friars. Copy the table and complete it to show how useful the monks and friars are to an *ordinary peasant* who works 8 to 12 hours a day, and lives in a small village, has never left the village, is *extremely* poor, goes to church regularly, cannot read or write and does not understand Latin. Use this code when you fill in the table:

✓✓ means 'Very Useful'
✓ means 'Useful'
✗ means 'Useless'

MONKS			FRIARS	
Activity	Usefulness		Activity	Usefulness
1 Singing prayers in Latin			1 Preaching a sermon in the village square in English	
2 Writing a page of a Latin book for the monastery library			2 Setting up a local school to teach villagers to read	
3 Entertaining visitors			3 Staying in people's houses	
4 Selling wool			4 Helping the sick	
5 Keeping quiet and thinking			5 Telling stories of places visited	

1 Use this table and the information on the previous page to explain why friars were popular with the peasants. What were the main differences between monks and friars?

Now read the documents below.

Look at what monks do for you in their war against the devil. Uncountable are the prayers, hymns, psalms and good works they perform daily. I advise you, noble earl, to build such a castle in your country, manned by monks against Satan.

Some friars drugged a man's drink until he could only say the word 'Yes'. They asked him if he would join their order. They then stole his goods, tore off his clothes and dressed him in a friar's habit. They were about to cut his hair off when he came to his senses and chased them out with the scissors.

2 Do these documents agree with the results of your table?

3 Would you say the writers were supporters of the friars? Explain.

Being a Friar

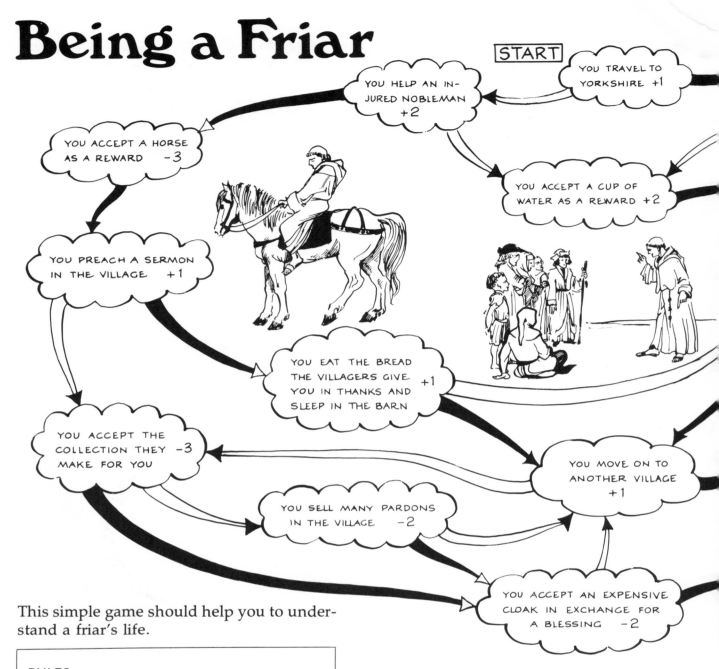

START

YOU TRAVEL TO YORKSHIRE +1

YOU HELP AN IN-JURED NOBLEMAN +2

YOU ACCEPT A HORSE AS A REWARD -3

YOU ACCEPT A CUP OF WATER AS A REWARD +2

YOU PREACH A SERMON IN THE VILLAGE +1

YOU EAT THE BREAD THE VILLAGERS GIVE YOU IN THANKS AND SLEEP IN THE BARN +1

YOU ACCEPT THE COLLECTION THEY MAKE FOR YOU -3

YOU MOVE ON TO ANOTHER VILLAGE +1

YOU SELL MANY PARDONS IN THE VILLAGE -2

YOU ACCEPT AN EXPENSIVE CLOAK IN EXCHANGE FOR A BLESSING -2

This simple game should help you to understand a friar's life.

RULES

1 Put some small token—coin, drawing-pin or counter—on the START box. You could make your own counter showing a picture of a friar or some part of a friar's costume.

2 You move your counter along the arrows from box to box. Note down *only* those events in the boxes on which you land. Note the score in the box.

3 When there are 2 exits from a box you toss a coin to decide your route. When you throw HEADS follow the arrow with a black head (➡); when you throw TAILS follow the arrow with a black tail (▰▷). Arrows which are all black MUST be followed.

4 You can play alone or in pairs sharing a board. The winner will be the best friar, that is the player with the highest score.

Answer these questions after you have played the game.

1 Look carefully at the boxes on the board with plus scores. Explain how each of the activities in the boxes would make someone a good friar.

2 Look carefully at the boxes on the board with minus scores. Explain how each of these breaks the rules of St Francis.

3 If you wished to attack or criticise friars, what sort of evidence would you hope to find?

4 Use the things that happened to you in the game to write a full and imaginative report to your abbot. Explain your successes and confess the temptations into which you fell. You can add

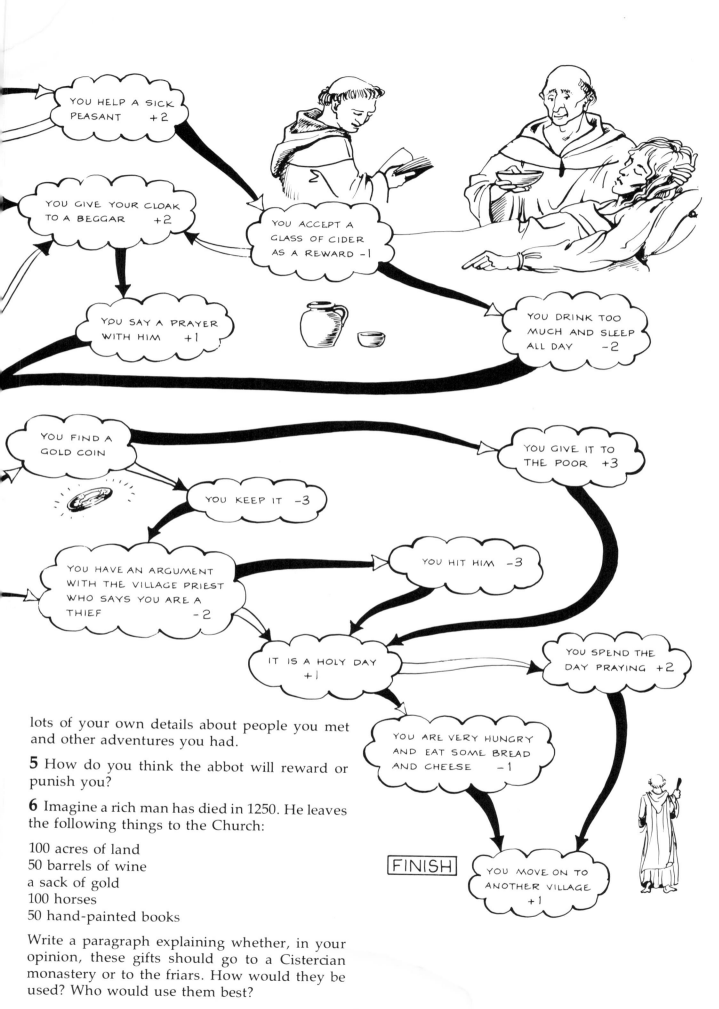

YOU HELP A SICK PEASANT +2

YOU GIVE YOUR CLOAK TO A BEGGAR +2

YOU ACCEPT A GLASS OF CIDER AS A REWARD -1

YOU SAY A PRAYER WITH HIM +1

YOU DRINK TOO MUCH AND SLEEP ALL DAY -2

YOU FIND A GOLD COIN

YOU GIVE IT TO THE POOR +3

YOU KEEP IT -3

YOU HAVE AN ARGUMENT WITH THE VILLAGE PRIEST WHO SAYS YOU ARE A THIEF -2

YOU HIT HIM -3

YOU SPEND THE DAY PRAYING +2

IT IS A HOLY DAY +1

YOU ARE VERY HUNGRY AND EAT SOME BREAD AND CHEESE -1

FINISH

YOU MOVE ON TO ANOTHER VILLAGE +1

lots of your own details about people you met and other adventures you had.

5 How do you think the abbot will reward or punish you?

6 Imagine a rich man has died in 1250. He leaves the following things to the Church:

100 acres of land
50 barrels of wine
a sack of gold
100 horses
50 hand-painted books

Write a paragraph explaining whether, in your opinion, these gifts should go to a Cistercian monastery or to the friars. How would they be used? Who would use them best?

Pilgrims and Relics

As you may have realised people did not travel very much in the Middle Ages. This was because most people had to work very hard to stay alive. Also the roads were difficult and dangerous.

One group of people who did travel were the pilgrims. These were people who went on pilgrimages to important religious centres. They went for many different reasons. Some went hoping to be cured of an illness. Some went to make up for a sinful life or some special crime they had committed. Some went for the excitement of going to a strange place or foreign land. Some were sent by a priest to make up for a particularly bad sin they had committed. This was called 'doing a penance'. The pilgrims went to places which were especially holy and contained important religious relics. These were things like pieces of the cross on which Jesus was crucified; part of his robe; a bone of a saint; and many other items of this sort.

By going on the journey the pilgrims hoped that the hardships of the journey, the sacrifice of giving up their normal life and the especially religious and holy atmosphere of the place of pilgrimage would help them. It was thought, for instance, that by touching the bones of a saint, someone who was ill could be cured.

Geoffrey Chaucer

The most famous description of a pilgrimage is found in *The Canterbury Tales* by Geoffrey Chaucer. Your teacher might like to read to you from this.

You will realise that pilgrims came from all sorts of places and did all sorts of jobs. You could make a list of them from Chaucer's book.

A reliquary

One of the most enjoyable parts of the pilgrimage must have been getting to know a group of strangers who came from different places. Pilgrims often stayed in the homes of people who were glad to give them food and shelter. At the place of pilgrimage the pilgrims would say prayers.

The bones and other holy remains became known as *relics*. Relics were often placed in special, beautifully decorated containers like the one shown on the right. Often they were kept in some great cathedral.

When the pilgrims reached the place of pilgrimage they could get a document to show they had been there. At the place of pilgrimage the pilgrim could buy all sorts of souvenirs, many of them supposed to be holy—things like badges and statues; bottles of holy water; and also relics, such as holy bones.

You can imagine that many of these places became rather like modern tourist centres. Many of them were quite large towns to begin with and they grew larger as more pilgrims came. Many people who did not mind how they made money would fake relics and sell them to pilgrims.

This is how a modern author describes Canterbury during a rather special medieval pilgrimage. Pilgrims came to Canterbury cathedral to visit the shrine that contained the bones of St Thomas Becket (see page 58).

"The carcasses of oxen and sheep were roasted whole and offered for sale. . . The inns had capons turning on spits . . . and mountains of loaves which the White and Brown Bakers had laboured for days to produce.

Mass was celebrated in all the churches and in the open on streets black with people as far as the eye could see. It took days for all the visitors to file through the cathedral.

Finally the pilgrims would visit the open booths in . . . High Street and Mercery Lane. Here tokens and pilgrim signs were on sale."

1 Explain what relics were.

2 Explain why people went on pilgrimages in the Middle Ages.

3 Explain why *each* of the following people might have liked to live in a town which was a centre for pilgrimages: a saddle-maker; a thief; an inn-keeper; a scribe (someone who can write well); a bootmaker; a tailor; a shopkeeper.

4 Explain why people were prepared to let pilgrims stay with them.

Places of Pilgrimage

In the Middle Ages there were many places that were places of pilgrimage because they contained some especially holy relics. The places where the saints had died were also very important. Some places were more important than others. Amongst these special places were Jerusalem, where Jesus spent much time and where he died, and Rome, where the Pope lived, which was the centre of the Christian world. St Peter, one of Jesus' chief disciples who became the first Pope, died in Rome.

For the people of England there were special shrines such as St Albans and Canterbury. Canterbury was the place where Thomas Becket had been killed by knights in 1170. Thomas was made a saint after his death.

PLACE	IMPORTANCE	CODE
St Patrick's Shrine	St Patrick, Patron Saint of Ireland. Drove snakes out of Ireland.	
Canterbury	St Thomas Becket killed here by armed knights in the cathedral.	
St Albans	Cathedral built on the spot where a Roman Soldier who was a Christian was put to death.	
Clermont	A spring of healing water rose here. Many 'incurable' people cured.	
Assisi	Birthplace of St Francis, founder of the friars. Loved animals.	
Compostella	Tomb of St James, one of the disciples of Jesus.	
Rome	The home of the Pope, head of the Church. St Peter and St Paul, who were the founders of the Christian Church, were put to death here. Also the place where many early Christians were thrown to the lions.	
Bethlehem	Birthplace of Jesus.	
Nazareth	Where Jesus spent his childhood.	

Read the section on places of pilgrimage on the opposite page. Look carefully at the map opposite and the table above.

1 (You may need an atlas for this exercise.) Draw the map in your book. Put the codes into their correct circles.

2 You are going on a pilgrimage. Plan a route which will allow you to visit 5 important shrines. Explain why you have chosen these shrines and mark the route on your map.

3 Which of these centres would have been considered the most important place of pilgrimage by people in the Middle Ages? Explain.

4 What do you think was necessary for someone to become a saint?

5 How do you think that Christians in England will react when they hear that Jerusalem has been captured by the Turks who are killing Christians and claiming the city for their religion (Islam)?

6 What action could English Christians take?

7 Suggest why a priest in the Middle Ages might order someone to go on *either* a pilgrimage to Rome *or* 3 pilgrimages to Canterbury.
The following 3 people all wish to go on a pilgrimage. Write a report suggesting
(a) how a pilgrimage would help them;
(b) where they should go;
(c) what they should do when they get there.

JOHN TAYLOR, a very rich cloth merchant from Lincoln. He is old and ill. He has not been able to attend church regularly but in recent years he has given much money to Lincoln Cathedral.

ALICE, the wife of a ploughman. She broke her arm recently and it has not set properly. It is very painful. She goes to church regularly. She is very poor.

SIR JUSTIN REDVERS, a knight who owns much land in Surrey. He has fought in France and Germany and killed many men. He is now getting too old for fighting and wants to retire quietly to his estates.

The Plague Arrives

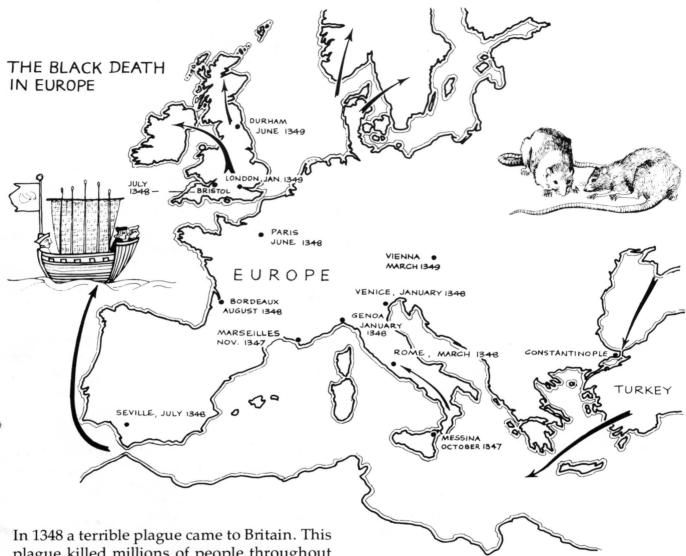

THE BLACK DEATH
IN EUROPE

DURHAM JUNE 1349

JULY 1348 —

LONDON, JAN. 1349

BRISTOL

PARIS JUNE 1348

EUROPE

VIENNA MARCH 1349

VENICE, JANUARY 1348

BORDEAUX AUGUST 1348

GENOA JANUARY 1348

MARSEILLES NOV. 1347

ROME, MARCH 1348

CONSTANTINOPLE

TURKEY

SEVILLE, JULY 1348

MESSINA OCTOBER 1347

In 1348 a terrible plague came to Britain. This plague killed millions of people throughout Europe. No one is really sure where it started but it reached Europe from Turkey.

People who caught the plague developed large boils under their arms. Their arms and legs became covered in black spots and they were unable to eat. They began to cough blood and within a few days they were dead. This plague became known as the Black Death.

Medieval people were terrified of it. There seemed to be no cure and it struck people down with no warning, rich and poor alike. What made it worse was that they knew the plague was coming but could do nothing to stop it. The worst effects of the Black Death were in the towns where people were packed closely together.

We know now that the Black Death was the bubonic plague. It is caused by a bacillus (germ) which lives in the fleas that are found on black rats. The fleas bite the rats, which infects their blood. The black rats seemed to have moved into Europe, possibly because weather conditions had changed. It is thought that the rats travelled on the many ships that crossed the Mediterranean Sea, bringing silks, spices and other goods from

Turkey. The Franciscan Friar, Michael of Piazza, described how the plague reached Sicily in 1347.

"At the beginning of October 1347, twelve Genoese galleys [ships] were fleeing from the vengeance which God was taking . . . they entered the harbour of Messina. In their bones they bore so deadly an illness and could not avoid death. The infection then spread to anyone who met the diseased."

1 Copy or trace the map. Using the dates shown draw arrows to show the route of the plague across Europe.

2 Using the map and information provided, work out how the Black Death spread from Italy to England, and how long it took.

3 Why were large sea-ports such as Bristol or Marseilles very likely starting points for the Black Death?

4 How does Michael of Piazza suggest the Black Death was carried?

~~~~~~

Medieval Explanations of the Black Death

Medieval people knew nothing about germs and infections. They believed that the Black Death was a punishment sent from God to remind people of His power. The Black Death was carried in a poisonous cloud, which spread to towns and countries where the people had forgotten God's commandments. Henry of Knighton wrote that God sent the Black Death to Leicester because the inhabitants spent too much time gambling, fighting and attending tournaments.

The poisonous cloud could be seen, and writers claimed that the following signs were all evidence that the Black Death had come:
  (a) A cloud of stinking smoke
  (b) Thunder and lightning
  (c) A rain of frogs and serpents
  (d) Poisoned earth and sea

The Black Death would then infect the whole area, and those people who caught the disease might pass it on by looking at or breathing on someone else. (Remember what Michael of Piazza wrote about the Genoese sailors.)

This explanation made sense to medieval people, because it fitted in with what they believed about God and punishment.

1 The table below shows some of the ways in which people tried to avoid being infected by the Black Death.

Copy the table into your books, then complete it by writing in the reason why medieval people believed they were saving themselves. Remember what you have read about medieval explanations of the Black Death.

2 Why did medieval people not believe the Black Death was caused by a bacillus (germ)?

3 Draw an illustration for a medieval book showing the causes of the Black Death.

4 Write a paragraph comparing the modern explanation of the Black Death with the medieval explanation.

Method	Reason
Smelling flowers or herbs	To avoid smelling the poison in the atmosphere
Praying	
Running away	
Locking yourself in your house	
Driving away strangers	
Buying relics	

61

The Plague Spreads

The Black Death spread very rapidly across Europe in 1348 and 1349. Doctors, who relied on herbal medicines and blood-letting, could do nothing to stop it. It is thought that in Britain about one-third of the total population were killed by the Black Death. The story was the same throughout Europe. Agnolo di Tura described the situation in the Italian city of Siena in 1348.

> "And in many places in Siena great pits were dug and piled deep with huge heaps of the dead . . . And I, Agnolo de Tura, called the Fat, buried my five children with my own hands, and so did many others likewise."

The Black Death in the Monasteries

Many people thought that the monasteries would not be affected by the Black Death. However, the disease could not be warded off by prayers or fasting, and most monks would die once their monastery was infected by the plague. This was because they shared dormitories, dining-rooms and work-places, and so the plague germs were passed on very rapidly. There was no one left to do the farm work after the Black Death had gone.

> "For in some religious houses, of twenty monks, scarce two survived. For, to say nothing of other monasteries, in the monastery of St Albans more than forty monks died in a short space of time . . . The plague was immediately followed by a murrain [illness] amongst the animals. At that time, money was lost, and for want of husbandmen [farmers] who were nowhere to be found, lands remained uncultivated. And such misery followed these misfortunes that the world never afterwards had the opportunity of returning to its former condition."

The Black Death in the Towns

Medieval towns contained hundreds of wooden houses crammed together in narrow streets. Filth and rubbish were often left in the streets, and the black rats found warmth and shelter in the houses, especially in the cellars. Once the disease was inside a town, it spread very rapidly indeed as all the inhabitants traded or worked together. In 1347, the population of London was 70,000. It is estimated that 30,000 Londoners died from the Black Death in 1348 and 1349.

The Black Death in Florence

> "In this extremity of our city's sufferings . . . the authority of laws was abused and all but totally dissolved, for lack of those who should have administered and enforced them, most of whom, like the rest of the citizens, were either dead or sick."

> "Many died daily or nightly in the public streets . . . It was the common practice of most of the neighbours . . . to drag the corpses out of the houses with their own hands, and lay them round in front of the doors."

> "Between March and July, upwards of a hundred thousand human beings lost their lives within the walls of the city of Florence. How many grand palaces, how many stately homes . . . once full of retainers, of lords, of ladies . . . were now left empty of all."

The citizens tried three ways of avoiding the plague:

> "Carrying in their hands flowers or fragrant herbs"
> "Others affirmed there was no better medicine than running away"
> "Or citizen avoided citizen, so among neighbours was scarce found any that showed fellow-feeling for another"

The Black Death in the Villages

The Black Death spread quickly into villages throughout Europe. In England, local priests, reeves, villeins and cottars were all killed by the plague, and there was hardly anyone left to do the farming work. Some villages never recovered at all and disappeared when the few survivors moved out after the Black Death.

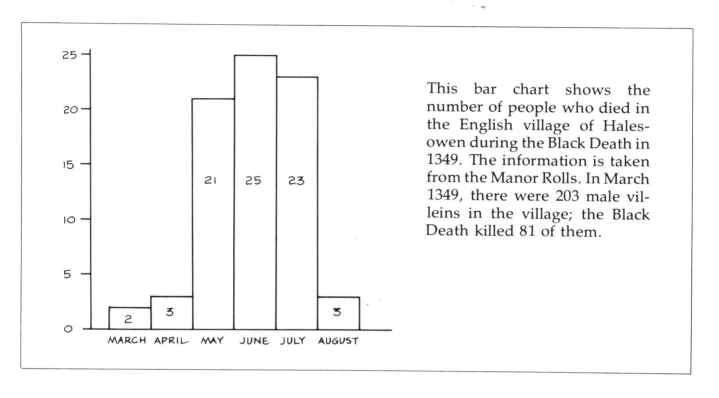

This bar chart shows the number of people who died in the English village of Halesowen during the Black Death in 1349. The information is taken from the Manor Rolls. In March 1349, there were 203 male villeins in the village; the Black Death killed 81 of them.

Results of the Black Death

An illustrated manuscript

Read pages 60-63 carefully before starting these exercises.

1 The picture above shows a page from an illustrated manuscript written in the Middle Ages. Small pictures in the margin and around the large capital letter emphasise the main points of the document.

Imagine that you are a novice monk producing an illustrated history of your monastery. Prepare an entry for the year 1349, assuming that the Black Death reached your monastery. Write one page only, and remember to design a large capital letter to start with.

2 Draw a map of the centre of a large medieval town or city. Include the following: a market place, two warehouses for storing grain, two butchers' shops, a road leading to the docks, a church and a graveyard. Explain how each of these would be a health hazard during an outbreak of the Black Death. (Remember how the Black Death was caused; and turn to page 9 for a map of a medieval town to help you.)

3 Imagine you are the reeve of Halesowen in 1349. Prepare a report for the lord outlining the problems faced by the villagers, and noting which jobs it will be difficult to get done.

4 Write and perform a play or improvisation to show the effects of the Black Death in a village, a town or a monastery.